W9-BIV-548

Kant and Theology

Other titles in the Philosophy and Theology series include:

Kant and Theology

Pamela Sue Anderson
and
Jordan Bell

t &t clark

Published by T&T Clark International
A Continuum Imprint
The Tower Building, 11 York Road, London SE1 7NX
80 Maiden Lane, Suite 704, New York, NY 10038

www.continuumbooks.com

British Library Cataloguing-in-Publication Data
A catalogue record for this book is available from the British Library

ISBN 13: 978-0-567-03414-4 (Hardback)
        978-0-567-03415-1 (Paperback)

Typeset by Newgen Imaging Systems Pvt Ltd, Chennai, India
Printed and bound in Great Britain by the MPG Books Group

[Kant's] island[1] *... dates from the eighteenth century, and marks an epoch: philosophers had previously been in the habit of offering us more joyful and directly desirable things at the end of the path of knowledge – holding out in their discourse a prospect of islands to which we might more happily transport ourselves. In considering then, the historical singularity of the Kantian island, one should also not forget the historical situation ... of a dated historical formation which strives to think ... on questions which are those of an epoch, and of a social category ...*

...[an] ancient happiness is no longer thinkable in the eighteenth century, as Kant does not fail to acknowledge, closing the Critique of Pure Reason, *for example, with some thoughts on nature as cruel stepmother, and on the veneration we owe the creator 'as much for what he has refused us as for what he has given us in recompense'. . . [the first* Critique*] points in this direction, but at the same time its metaphor annuls this and organizes a seduction into renunciation by depicting an island already discovered ... A restoration of paradise on earth, through the work and progress of the ... sciences, is declared possible and even already begun, despite and notwithstanding everything – even if the system cannot found this hope on reason. But without this hope, can there be a* Critique of Pure Reason?[2]

Contents

Contents

Kant and Theology

by Pamela Sue Anderson and Jordan Bell

The philosophy of Kant is widely acknowledged to have had a major impact on theology. However, due to the vastness and complexity of Kant's philosophical system, contemporary theologians and ethicists tend to steer clear of his actual writings and often exhibit a misunderstanding of his central ideas on reason, morality and religion. Anderson and Bell aim to make Kant accessible again to new generations of students and to challenge twenty-first-century academics to return to Enlightenment rationality. *Kant and Theology* takes a fresh look at freedom, evil and human autonomy in Kant's *Critique of Pure Reason, Groundwork of the Metaphysics of Morals* and *Critique of Practical Reason*, as well as his *Religion Within the Boundaries of Mere Reason* and 'An Answer to the Question: What is Enlightenment?', demonstrating how these core texts can inform debates about a range of topics including salvation, heaven, ritual practices and the role of reason for religious people today. Teachers of theology, philosophy of religion, ethics and feminist philosophy will find novel insights for solving practical and theoretical disputes over what place human agents and 'moral religion' have in a world shaped by ever-new scientific and cross-cultural advances. This book in the *Philosophy for Theologians* series includes a selective biography of Kant's life and theology, four main chapters and a conclusion focusing on critical reception of Kant.

The authors of *Kant and Theology* offer two acknowledgements. First, they would like to thank the Oxford philosopher A. W. Moore for introducing us to each other as colleagues who could share a passion for the philosophy of Kant. Second, they would like to thank their Oxford D. Phil supervisors: Pamela owes a debt to Alan Montefiore and Jordan to J. D. Kenyon who each in the 1980s and in the 1990s, respectively, encouraged critical engagement with Kant. Of course, any problems which remain in the present reading of Kant are their own.

Kant: His Life and Theology

Immanuel Kant was born on 22 April 1724 in the city of Königsberg in Eastern Prussia on the Baltic Sea. The name which the *Old Prussian Almanac* associated with this date was 'Emanuel'.[1] In accordance with this Kant was baptized Emanuel, meaning 'God is with him'. Kant took great pride in this name, and often commented on its meaning, even in old age.[2] It gave him great confidence and comfort throughout his life. It is, however, notable and perhaps fitting that, even in the matter of his given name, the great scholar would not accept things uncritically. Around 1746, Kant changed his name from Emanuel to 'Immanuel', thinking the latter to be a truer rendition of the Hebrew word.

Kant throughout his life famously never travelled outside of Eastern Prussia. But while Königsberg would not have been deemed the most likely place for one of the greatest revolutions in modern philosophy to originate, neither would it be right to view the city as a backwater. Originally founded in 1255 by the Teutonic Knights, it had grown to be a highly prominent town. Situated on the Baltic, at the mouth of the River Pregel, it was an important trading port, with close links to countries in the Eastern Baltic, as well as England. There were also close connections, of course, with Berlin, the capital of Prussia. Königsberg was the home of significant Mennonite, French-speaking Huguenot and Jewish communities. The cosmopolitan nature of the town allowed for greater social mobility than in many other German cities.

Kant himself came from a family of modest means. His father, Johann Georg, was a harness-maker. Emanuel was the

1

fourth of nine children, three of whom died in infancy. It was his mother, Anna Regina, who first encouraged him towards an academic education. Her death, when Emanuel was only thirteen, greatly affected him. Throughout his life, Kant had nothing but good to say of his parents. In 1797, he wrote in a letter, that

> my two parents (from the class of tradesmen) were
> perfectly honest, decent and orderly. They did not leave
> me a fortune (but neither did they leave me any debts).
> Moreover, they gave me an education that could not have
> been better when considered from the moral point of view.
> Every time I think of this I am touched by feelings
> of the highest gratitude.[3]

Kant's mother and father were deeply religious people and strongly influenced by the Pietist movement within the Lutheran Church. Pietism may be seen as a reaction against the formality of the Lutheran orthodoxy. The highly professional clergy were seen as too dryly intellectual and too concerned with the outward adherence of their flock to theological doctrines rather than to their inner spiritual well-being. They were also perceived as being too closely allied to the gentry and little concerned with the less educated people. Pietism may be seen as originating with the publication of Philipp Jakob Spener's *Pia desideria* (*Pious Desires*), published in 1675.[4] Rather than viewing Christian faith as 'a set of doctrinal propositions', Pietists saw it as 'a living relationship with God'.[5] They encouraged independent Bible study and personal devotion, and they emphasized the great importance of the personal experience of radical conversion or rebirth, preceded by struggle and repentance. This inner and living faith was to be reconfirmed daily with acts of obedience to God's commandments. Opposed to an overly intellectual attitude towards faith, Pietism sought to represent religions as a matter of the heart. In services, the signing of hymns, linked with appealing tunes, was greatly encouraged by Pietists in order to inspire moral and religious commitment among the people in the pews.

Although primarily a German movement Pietism has had a profound impact on the wider world. For example, Pietism was an important source of spiritual inspiration for John Wesley. In particular, it is said that Wesley was 'touched' by the 'fervently emotional' Christ-centred religion, which characterized the radical Pietism of Count Nikolaus Ludwig von Zinzendorf (1700–1760), and Wesley translated some of Zinzendorf's Pietist hymns into English.[6]

One reason why Pietism successfully spread in Prussia is that it was supported by King Frederick William I (who ruled from 1713 to 1740). With his agenda of forging a strong centralized state and effective administration, he used the Pietist movement to help him get his reforms through. As his reforms were against the interests of the landed gentry (who themselves were allied to the Lutheran Orthodoxy) supporting Pietism gave him a populist way of indirectly weakening their power. The reform of the education system encouraging the schooling of the children of the poor, in spite of opposition from the landed gentry was one of the King's aims which received much Pietist support. In Königsberg, the school to which the young Emanuel was sent in 1732, the *Collegianum Fredericianum*, was founded and run on strict Pietist principles. Being admitted to the school was a crucial step in the academic and social advancement of the son of a harness-maker.

While Kant admired his own parents' sincerely held religious spiritualism, his experience at school of Pietism in its institutional aspect gave rise to his having a life-long antipathy to this movement. As a Pietistic institution, the *Collegianum* aimed not just to educate the intellects of its pupils but also to educate their wills. It aimed to break the natural and worldly wilfulness of the children and to educate them on the first step of the struggle of contrition (which it was hoped the children would voluntarily continue for themselves). While all schools emphasized religious observance, the focus on the individual pupil's struggle was an identifiably Pietistic feature of the institution. It was this feature which Kant found highly oppressive.

While Pietists did not oppose corporal punishment, other ways of disciplining pupils were ideally preferred. When a pupil was to attend communion, the *Collegium* required him to write a report on the state of his own soul. On the basis of this, a school supervisor would judge whether the pupil was spiritually ready to take communion. In addition, the supervisor would compare a pupil's own reports with those written by the teacher. If they were significantly different, the pupil would be admonished.[7] Kant's dislike in later life for introspection may be traced to this being forced to write these reports on his inner life. Kant remarked that such attempts at observing 'oneself' could easily lead to insanity.[8]

While he admired true conviction, Kant thought that the school's emphasis on piety encouraged the pretence of conviction. He was unwilling to follow any of his school fellows in adapting themselves to affected piety. Although it is possible to identify many positive influences which Pietism had on Kant's philosophy of religion (such as his recognition of the importance of moral struggle and conversion), almost all of Kant's explicit references to Pietism are negative.[9] Crucially, the mature Kant's philosophy rejected any religion based upon feeling or sentiment alone. It is essential to his thinking that true religion should, rather, be based upon reason. In addition, we may track to his experiences at school Kant's aversion to petitionary prayer which he viewed as the 'wheedling of God'.[10] Kant thought that the singing of hymns, and outward religious observances such as church attendance would easily degenerate into conventionalism. Even in later life when his University duties obliged him to preside at religious services, he avoided this by claiming to be indisposed.

In 1740, Kant became a student at the University of Königsberg. This was a significant year, for in it, Frederick William I died and was succeeded by his son Frederick the

Great as King. Kant had a strong admiration for Frederick. Kant even in some way identified with him, seeing parallels between his life and with Frederick's resistance to his father's brutal attempts to change his character. One of Frederick's first acts in power was to recall the philosopher Christian Wolff from exile, which had been imposed on him by Frederick William I, and to reinstall him as a professor in the University of Halle. This was an act of symbolic support for the *Aufklärung* movement. Many years later in his, 'An Answer to the Question: What is Enlightenment?' (1784), Kant suggested that the age of Enlightenment might even be called 'the century of Frederick'.[11]

At University, Kant initially studied Latin literature. But he later studied mathematics, metaphysics and natural science. He was exposed to a wide range of material, including the works of Wolff and the ideas of Isaac Newton. One of Kant's most prominent professors was Martin Knutzen (1713–1751). Kant was not regarded by Knutzen as one of his better students, and this might have been a factor in the remarkably slow rate at which Kant's academic career developed. After completing his University studies and after the death of his father in 1746, Kant left Königsberg and from 1748 to 1754 worked as a private tutor in households in East Prussia. He was fortunate in his employers, among whom were the influential and aristocratic Keyserlingk family, with whom Kant maintained a long-term friendship. Although his employers regarded Kant highly, his own estimation of his skills as a private tutor was as low as could be – reportedly thinking 'he was probably the worst private teacher, *Hofmeister*, who had ever lived'.[12]

When Kant returned to Königsberg, opportunities opened for him at the University. He submitted his dissertation for the degree in philosophy and in 1755 became a University Lecturer (or *Privatdozent*). Although this post gave him the right to teach at the University, it had no salary attached to it. He had to earn his money from the fees which students paid to him for attending his lectures. Not only did he lecture a minimum of sixteen hours a week, but he taught a remarkable range of subjects – from logic, metaphysics, ethics and natural theology to mathematics, physics, chemistry and geography. He was a highly popular speaker easily filling his lecture halls. On top of lecturing Kant also found time to publish.

During Kant's period as *Privatdozent*, great political events were afoot. In 1756, Frederick the Great marched his troops into Saxony. This started the Seven Years' War (1756–1763) in which Prussia (allied with Great Britain) fought against Austria, France, Russia, Sweden and Saxony. Although ultimately vict-orious, the war was a highly costly one for Prussia. Königsberg itself was occupied by Russia from 1758 to 1762. Surprisingly, this period of occupation was a good time for Kant. Many Russian commanders were highly supportive of the cultural and intellectual life of Königsberg. Officers attended his lec-tures and he even gave private tuition to some. Not only did this lead to his finances improving, but also his being invited to many dinners and parties of influential people. At this time, Kant became admired as a person of elegance, intelligence and wit. In particular, he continued to be invited to dinners at the estate of Count Keyserlingk. The Countess, who herself had a great interest in philosophy and had translated Wolff into French, almost always seated Kant in the place of honour next to her at the dinner table. The Countess was greatly admired by Kant. Otherwise the society of a university lecturer at that time was almost exclusively made up of men. Kant twice came close to marriage. However, both times he dithered too long before taking the final step, worrying about whether he had the money to support a family, and the chance to marry passed him by. It is said, he joked, 'when he could have benefited from marriage, he could not afford it, and when he could afford it, he could no longer have benefited from it'.[13]

One of the most significant friendships that he made in his life was with Joseph Green (1727–1786). Green was a suc-cessful but eccentric English merchant living in Königsberg. In spite of his commercial success, he was more interested in intellectual matters than in business. Highly educated Green was described as 'more of a scholar than a merchant'.[14] They met around the year 1765 and quickly became very close friends. The bachelor Green led a peculiarly ordered life. Kant was a regular visitor to Green's house, but always would leave at seven o'clock exactly, due to Green's insistence on punctuality. Once Kant and Green arranged to take a carriage into the countryside, they agreed to leave at eight a.m. On the dot of eight, as Kant had not yet arrived, Green left without him. Shortly afterwards, Green passed Kant on the road but in spite of Kant's signalling he refused to stop; to do so would be counter to Green's rules and punctuality.[15] Green's living his life according to order and rules, or maxims, rather than according to the desires of the moment, had a great influence on Kant. Not only did Kant's life become much more methodical over time, abandoning the social whirl of his earlier years, Green's insistence on the centrality of maxims for action might well have had an important influence on Kant's subsequent practical writings on moral maxims. Kant also became a good friend of Robert Motherby, Green's business assistant and later his partner in the firm. Kant invested most of his money in the Green and Motherby company. This investment led to his being comfortably off in later life, although he never earned a high salary.

In 1770, Kant finally became a professor at the University of Königsberg. He had shortly before declined similar opportunities at Erlangen and Jena. The security afforded by this appointment gave Kant some respite from his hectic *Privatdozent* workload. The decade of 1770 to 1780 is known as Kant's 'silent years', for in this period he published very little. Throughout this decade, Kant was slowly developing the ideas which were eventually to constitute the *Critique of Pure Reason*. A typical Kantian day at this point of his life would have been roughly as follows. He would be woken up at five a.m. by his servant, Martin Lampe. He would drink tea and smoke a pipe and after that work on his lectures until seven a.m. His lectures would begin at seven a.m. and end by eleven a.m. He would then work on his writings until lunchtime. After lunch, he would take a walk and spend the rest of the afternoon with Green. After going back home, he would do a little more work and reading before bed.

Kant's *Critique of Pure Reason* finally came out in 1781, when he was 56 years old. Although initial critical reception of this book was cool, as the decade of the 1780s progressed, the great originality of the work was recognized and Kant's fame as a philosopher spread. In the late 1780s, the first *Critique* became the focus of German philosophical discourse. Critics tried to understand it and progress from it. Many new publications followed, including the *Prolegomena to any Future Metaphysics* (1783), *Groundwork of the Metaphysics of Morals* (1785), a second edition of *Critique of Pure Reason* (1787), *Critique of Practical Reason* (1788) and *Critique of the Power of Judgment* (1790).

Frederick the Great died in 1786 and was succeeded by his nephew, the much more conservative, Frederick William II as King of Prussia. Whereas Frederick the Great had favoured toleration and religious liberalism, his successor had long been shocked by the unorthodoxy and scepticism which had been allowed to flourish. Frederick William II appointed Johann Christoph Wöllner, Minister of Ecclesiastical Affairs. In 1788, Wöllner issued two edicts, with the aim of enforcing strict orthodoxy upon religious clergy and academics in what they preached and taught in public. These edicts were highly unpopular among Prussian intellectuals, who feared that they might lose their positions. This climate of censorship continued throughout the years of the French Revolution, which began in 1789.

Kant was sympathetic with the ideals of the Revolution and openly declared himself 'a republican'. In his 1795 essay, 'Perpetual Peace', however, he indicated that a limited constitutional monarchy, in which the ruler sees himself as the servant of the state, would fall under the category of republican. Direct problems with the censors, however, did not fall on Kant until

Introduction

he tried to publish his *Religion within the Boundaries of Mere Reason*. In 1792, he sent two parts of this book to Berlin to be published, explicitly asking for them to be sent to the Berlin office of censorship. The first of the two was passed by the censors (as it was thought to be essentially a philosophical piece and not for the wider public), but the second was rejected, since it was deemed to be too theological. Kant swiftly responded by sending the whole of the *Religion* to the philosophical faculty of Jena which had its own independent censorship authority. It was passed there and the *Religion* in its entirety was published in 1793. Kant even put out a second edition in the following year.

Kant's bold evasion of the Berlin restrictions was a clear affront to Wöllner and his censors. Matters could not stop there. In 1794, Wöllner wrote to Kant, in the name of the King, castigating him for his misuse of his philosophy in distorting the teachings of Christianity. He was commanded, on pain of unpleasant consequences, to cease all future teaching and writing on religion, which did not conform to Christian orthodoxy. Kant's position at the University was at stake, since he held his professorship at the pleasure of the King. In the end, Kant submitted to the King's will. He defended himself against all charges that he had attacked religion in his lectures and writings, but agreed 'as Your Majesty's loyal subject' to refrain from all future public discourse, lectures and writings on religion.[16] That, it seemed, was that. However, the phrase 'as Your Majesty's loyal subject' turned out subsequently to be crucial. For the next several years Kant kept strictly to his promise. He did not shy away from writing about controversial subjects, such as politics, but he avoided religion.

In 1797, however, the King died and was succeeded by Frederick William III. Kant took this opportunity to publish a piece concerning religion, which he had composed some years earlier. It was called, *The Conflict of the Faculties* (1798) and disputed the relationship between the Faculty of Theology and other university faculties, including that of philosophy. In the

9

preface to the piece, Kant argues that his promise to refrain from religious writings was a personal one to King Frederick William II (as indicated by 'as Your Majesty's loyal subject') rather than to the state of Prussia. As King Frederick William II was no longer living, his promise no longer stood. Kant had kept his word. Just. Kant retired from lecturing in 1796 and although he continued to publish until 1800, he grew weaker and suffered from illness. He died in 1804, not long before his eightieth birthday. His grave still stands outside the cathedral in Königsberg – which is now called Kaliningrad. At his death, he was seen to have left German philosophy with a dilemma. Should Kant's work be rejected, accepted or gone beyond. The same dilemma faces readers of Kant today.

Chapter 1

Themes from Transcendental Idealism

Introducing Kant's *Critique of Pure Reason*

What is it that makes a philosopher great? It might be suggested that great philosophers are those who put forward doctrines that reveal the truth to us. But although proposing true doctrines might help, this suggestion cannot be quite right since we might want to call two philosophers great whose doctrines completely oppose each other. We would be closer to the mark in calling a philosopher great who gives us the means to answer central philosophical problems in a radically new (and inspiring) way. They make us see things in a new way and hence, shift the course of subsequent philosophical debate. Now, if this suggestion is correct, then Kant is a very great philosopher, for he radically and inspiringly shifted the debates not in one, but many philosophical areas. The way that we talk about, for example, metaphysics, epistemology, the philosophy of mathematics, morality, aesthetics and religion have all been profoundly influenced by Kant.

Kant's influence has been so broad that there is a strong tendency among scholars of Kant to specialize in one branch of his philosophy to the neglect of others. Kant's philosophy may be divided into his theoretical philosophy and his practical philosophy. His theoretical philosophy is largely expounded in Kant's greatest book, the *Critique of Pure Reason*; this focuses on questions (or it is thought) relating to science, mathematics and epistemology. His practical philosophy focuses on morality, aesthetics and religion. There is a tendency among Kant scholars who study his theoretical philosophy to neglect his practical philosophy (and vice versa). This limiting of one's study is quite understandable given the complexity of Kant's thought. However, this trend of separation is regrettable. If the two sides of Kant's philosophy were separable, then you might expect what Kant has to say in a 'Critique of Pure Theoretical Reason' to be of little interest to a theologian whose primary interest is Kant's practical philosophy. But this is very far from the truth. The *Critique of Pure Reason* is of great interest to theologians and ethicists, for it is the book where Kant lays the foundation for all the rest of his philosophy.

The *Critique of Pure [Theoretical] Reason* might well be described as the book where Kant explores the foundations of scientific knowledge. He explores what preconditions must be assumed to hold if we are to have scientific knowledge. This description is an accurate one; however, it gives the impression that Kant's focus in this book is solely on science. That Kant had much broader interests in writing the *Critique of Pure Reason* is what makes his master work so deeply fascinating. The book is a *Critique* of theoretical reason; that is, it is an examination of the limits of reason in its scientific aspect. Here Kant explores what it is possible for us to have scientific knowledge of and what it is not. But in describing what we cannot have scientific knowledge of, Kant is committing himself to saying that we can talk meaningfully about it. There is more to human life than science. Morality, freedom, God and religion may be outside the realms of science and yet we can (and perhaps must) still talk about them. We cannot have scientific knowledge of such things, but we can still *think* them. What is outside the bounds of theoretical, or scientific, reason might still be accessible to our practical reason. Thus the project of the *Critique of Pure Reason* might be seen as the making room for the possibility of morality and religion. Even though it lies outside the bounds of theoretical reason,

Kant is implicitly allowing for another form of human reason – namely, practical reason.

In this chapter, we shall explore how it is that Kant lays the foundation for the possibility of morality and religion. In particular, we shall examine Kant's famous doctrine of transcendental idealism and show how he addresses the age old problem of free will. Kant regards free will as a precondition for morality and religion.

The Problem of Metaphysics

Kant lived at a time when empirical science had made extra-ordinary advances. The theories of Newton and others apparently allowed us to explore and predict the movements not only of planets but also of everyday things with which we come into contact. This evident substantial progress in science seemed to contrast with an embarrassing lack of progress in such fields as philosophy and theology. Far from making progress, metaphysical debates (those beyond empirical science) seemed to be stuck in a mire of endless inconclusive disputes. A central question which exercised Kant in the *Critique of Pure Reason* was whether knowledge in metaphysics is possible at all. Kant answers this question by saying that metaphysical knowledge is possible, because it is necessary in order for us to have any experience at all. How does he reach this conclusion? Let us consider the most ordinary everyday experiences. When asked what sort of things we have knowledge of, a very natural commonsense response would be that we have knowledge, for example, of trees, chairs, tables and other creatures around us in the world.

The philosophers who provide us with the simplest account of how we have experience of these things are empiricists, such as John Locke. According to empiricists, how it is that we have knowledge of chairs, tables, etc. is essentially an empirical or scientific question. We, the human perceivers of the objects, are just scientific objects ourselves – like the things that we are observing. Like a piece of putty in which an impression is left by a falling pebble, so are our minds causally acted upon, and left with impressions, by the things that we see. Just as there is a scientific story to be told about how the pebble makes an impression in the putty, so there is a parallel story as to how a mind receives an impression (and knowledge) of something that it sees. Both stories are told in terms of the brute causes of nature. An important element of the empiricist account of experiential knowledge is that we are, just like the piece of putty, essentially passive receivers.

An advantage of this empiricist account of experiential knowledge is its simplicity. It reduces what might be seen as a philosophical question to a scientific question. How the mind has knowledge of external things is a scientific or empirical question. The precise causal mechanism by which impressions in the mind are brought about by external objects is a matter for scientific investigation. Kant, however, rejects the empiricist account. For Kant, this explanation is not just simple, but simplistic. It fails to do justice to the highly complicated and remarkable nature of human knowledge. Knowledge, Kant claims, cannot be a purely passive affair, like the reception of an impression by a piece of putty. Experiential knowledge *means* something to us. Yet the impression does not mean anything to the putty. It just happens to it. Kant's response is to say that our experiential knowledge cannot be a mere happening. It must be (in part) an active thing that we perform. We, as scientists, do not just read things off from the world; we read things *into* the world. Only then can we make sense of the fact that our experiential knowledge is of significance to us.

This move radically shifts Kant away from the simple empiri-cist theory of knowledge and gives rise to his far more complex theory. The things that we read into the world are the necessary conditions for knowledge to make sense to us humans. They are our metaphysical knowledge. They are what are necessary to get empirical scientific knowledge underway. To count as metaphysical knowledge, the judgement must not be derivable from empirical science; it must be *a priori*. The judgement must also not be a purely trivial analytic claim like the tautology, 'all dogs are dogs'. Instead it must be substantial in content. 'Synthetic' as a technical term is used here by Kant to describe content which has arisen out of a process of bringing together two contrasting elements: that is, the synthesis of an intuitive element and a conceptual element. 'Intuition' is what allows us to speak of particular things, while 'concepts' are what allow us to classify things and speak of objects in general. Kant calls our faculty of intuition, 'sensibility', and our faculty of conceptualization, 'understanding'.

Both the intuitive and the conceptual elements are required for any knowledge at all, whether empirical or metaphysical. In Kant's famous words,

> Without sensibility no object would be given to us,
> without understanding no object would be thought.
> Thoughts without content are empty, intuitions
> without concepts are blind.[1]

This fusion of sensibility and understanding shows that Kant's account of knowledge is far more complex than that given by the empiricists. To have knowledge, there must be individual things for us to conceptualize. What confers individuality on things for us humans, according to Kant, is space and time. As Kant puts it, space and time are the human forms of intuition. We humans can describe an object as much as we like, by listing the concepts under which it falls, but we can never be sure that we have picked out that individual. There might be another object satisfying those concepts; for instance, in a mirror image world. To pick out the individual, we humans need to do something deeply un-conceptual and point at the thing; that is, to specify its spatial-temporal location. This is how we humans confer individuality on things. Whether there are other beings, albeit radically different from us – such as God – who does it in another way, is another matter.

So, in order for us to have any knowledge at all (which we evidently do have), we must be able to recognize the individuality of things. This, in turn, for us humans means that we must recognize them as being spatio-temporally located. Space and time are preconditions for any human experiential knowledge. Now, according to Kant, there is a vast body of truths embedded in space and time; namely, those of geometry and arithmetic. The geometrical claim that the sum of the internal angles of a triangle equals two right angles tells us a substantial feature of the structure of space. The arithmetical claim, '1 + 1 = 2', similarly tells us something substantial about the structure of time. If space and time must be presupposed for any experiential knowledge, so must the body of truths which constitute geometry and arithmetic. These truths are according to Kant both *a priori* and synthetic (no mere tautologous play of concepts) and, as such may count as examples of metaphysical knowledge.

There are many other things of which, in the course of the *Critique of Pure Reason*, Kant argues that we have metaphysical knowledge. One of these is causation. The philosopher David Hume famously argued that while humans can observe the movement of one billiard ball hitting another and the other moving off, they cannot observe the causal force itself jumping from one billiard bell to the other. As an empiricist, he concluded that since we cannot scientifically observe it, we can have no knowledge of the causal link between the balls. This gives rise to a worrying scepticism. We all *believe* there to be a causal link, but cannot claim knowledge of it. In response to Hume, Kant argued that although we have no *empirical* knowledge of the causal link, we can have metaphysical knowledge of it. This is because the claim that there is a causal link between the billiard balls is a synthetic *a priori* claim. It is a substantial claim and is required for us to have any experiential knowledge at all. Just as the truths of geometry and arithmetic are built into our human faculty of sensibility, so causality is a requirement of our faculty of understanding.

Thus, according to Kant, metaphysical knowledge is possible. Whether Kant is right in claiming metaphysical knowledge of the particular things that he does is the subject of much heated philosophical debate. That is outside the scope of the chapter. Our purpose is to outline and explain the radical ambition of his theory.

Transcendental Idealism

Kant here won for us what seems a great victory. He has shown that we do have knowledge in metaphysics. In particular, we can know *a priori* the nature of space and time. But in order to understand fully how this metaphysical knowledge is possible, we must turn to Kant's great and radical core theory of the *Critique of Pure Reason* — transcendental idealism. At the heart of this theory is the distinction between appearances and things in themselves.

Kant has argued that we have *a priori* knowledge of the world of space and time. But, how is this so? On the simple empiricist theory, such *a priori* knowledge would be impossible. On this theory, the world operates independently of us. If we wish to gain knowledge of it, our minds must set about empirically investigating it. But then any knowledge which we gained of it would be empirical and not *a priori*; it would lack certainty. So, if Kant wishes to claim that we do have *a priori* knowledge of the world of space and time, then he must reject the empiricist assumption that in gaining knowledge of spatio-temporal things, the mind must conform itself to objects.

Instead of this Kant proposes an alternative theory.

Hitherto it has been assumed that all our knowledge must conform to objects. But all attempts to ascertain anything about them *a priori* by concepts, and thus extend our knowledge, came to nothing on this assumption. Let us try, then, whether we may not make better progress in the tasks of metaphysics if we assume that objects must conform to our knowledge. This at all events accords better with the possibility which we are seeking, namely of a knowledge of objects a priori, which would determine something about them before they are given to us.[2]

We can have *a priori* knowledge of spatio-temporal objects. But this is achieved at the expense of infusing these spatio-temporal objects with the assumptions of our own minds. This is the startling doctrine of transcendental idealism. As Kant would put it, space and time are transcendentally ideal. Spatio-temporal objects are not entirely independent of us after all. We have *a priori* access to them because we made them conform to the necessary conditions of our knowledge.

This extraordinary shift of philosophical perspective is likened by Kant to that proposed by Copernicus. The shift from the Ptolomeic worldview that the sun revolves around the earth to the Copernican theory that the earth revolves around the sun is a simple one, but with radical consequences to our understanding of the world. Kant thinks that this simple shift from the worldview of a passive self, receiving information from the world to an active self, infusing the world with its own assumptions is just as radical a revolution in thought. Kant would deny that the world of space and time is created by us. It is not brought into existence by the mere power of thought. Rather he is saying that in order to know things we must subject those things to the *a priori* conditions of knowledge. The commentator Frederick Copleston draws a rough analogy with a person who views the world through red tinted spectacles.[3] This person does not create the things seen in the way that God creates things. On the contrary, there must be something already there in order for the glasses to have any effect. But still everything that the person sees is infused with her or his own impositions.

In some sense, then, the world infused with our assumptions of space, time and causation is a world of appearance. It is to be contrasted with things as they are in themselves. Although Kant has been at pains to argue that we can have knowledge, it can now be seen that the only things that we can know are mere appearances and not things as they really are in themselves. Is this a hollow victory? There is a live debate among scholars of Kant as to what this distinction between appearances and things in themselves amounts to.[4] Is Kant literally positing two worlds of things: a world of spatio-temporal causal phenomena and another shadowy world of mysterious things in themselves? On this understanding, Kant is making an ontological distinction.

Those who adopt this ontological account of Kant's distinction typically find Kant's theory of transcendental idealism highly problematical, and they tend to be quite unsympathetic to transcendental idealism. If things that we can have scientific knowledge of literally form a different world to that of things as they really are in themselves, then any scientific discoveries that we make are irrelevant to reality. Indeed, we might wonder whether it might not be better for us simply to abandon all talk of things as they are in themselves. While we have direct knowledge of the world of appearances (phenomena), the world of things as they are in themselves (noumena) is inaccessible and hence irrelevant to us. Many scholars who interpret transcendental idealism in this way think that Kant's references to things as they are in themselves are highly problematical and at best irrelevant.

There is, however, another – more sympathetic – interpretation of transcendental idealism. According to this, speaking of appearances (phenomena) and things as they are in themselves (noumena) is not to distinguish between two worlds of things, but rather to distinguish between two ways of considering the same things. It is not an ontological distinction, but rather an epistemological one. This epistemological account may be called the two-aspect interpretation of transcendental idealism, as opposed to the two-world interpretation.

We may well want to view objects from the standpoint of science, or what Kant calls the standpoint of theoretical reason. In this case, we regard things as objects of knowledge and accordingly imbue them with the necessary conditions for them to be objects of our knowledge. But we might also want to consider them independently of the conditions of knowledge. In such a case, we would call them things in themselves. But they are the same things that we are considering in both cases. Why should we speak of things in themselves at all? At the heart of transcendental idealism is the idea that we read things *into* the world not just read things *off* from the world. We must read into the world the properties or principles which are necessary to view things as objects of science. But the question naturally arises as to what the things are that we are reading principles into. If we answer 'things in themselves', we mean things considered independently of the conditions of knowledge. In order to get the theory of transcendental idealism off the ground, we have to make some reference to things in themselves.

The debate between the two-aspect and the two-world interpretations of transcendental idealism is a lively and a current one. We shall not attempt to resolve it. But in the subsequent course of this book, the more sympathetic and – we believe – more rewarding two-aspect interpretation is the one that we shall choose to adopt.[5]

At this point, we would like to offer four separate quotations – each is from Kant's first *Critique* – to illustrate how Kant makes transcendental idealist distinctions. Note the use of metaphors and imagery, in presenting his transcendental idealism and its implications for epistemology, morality, religion; the 'human standpoint' on 'the world' holds all of these together. The following quotations help to create the picture, which is our starting point, for the distinctions between knowing and thinking,[6] and between theoretical and practical reason:

> . . . an *island*, enclosed by nature itself within unalterable limits . . . surrounded by a wide and stormy ocean, the

native home of illusion, where many a fog bank and
many a swiftly melting iceberg give the deceptive
appearance of farther shores, deluding the adventurous
seafarer ever anew with empty hopes . . . Before we
venture on this sea . . . it will be well to begin by casting
a glance upon the map of the land which we are about
to leave, and to enquire, first, whether we cannot in any
case be *satisfied* with what it contains . . . and, secondly,
by what title we possess even this domain, and can
consider ourselves as *secure* against all opposing claims.[7]

[T]hough I cannot *know*, I can yet *think* freedom;
that is to say, the representation of it is at least not
self-contradictory, provided due account be taken of
our critical distinction between the two modes of
representation, the sensible and the intellectual, and
of the resulting limitation of the pure concepts of
understanding and of the principles which flow from
them.[8] . . .

Morality does not, indeed, require that *freedom* should
be understood but only that it should not contradict
itself, and so should at least allow of being *thought*.[9]
It is solely from the *human* standpoint that we can
speak of space.[10]

From Theoretical Reason to Practical Reason

Kant has argued that we have synthetic *a priori* knowledge. In
other words, we have metaphysical knowledge of causation,
geometry and arithmetic, and these form the bedrock of science. These are necessary assumptions, in order for us to obtain
scientific knowledge at all – that is, to engage in theoretical
reasoning. So, we can have metaphysical knowledge after all.
But the heart of what might be called metaphysics has so far
eluded us. None of our discovered metaphysical principles
have anything to say about what Kant regards as the chief
metaphysical problems of God, freedom and immortality.

Ideas, such as 'God'[11], lie outside the scope of scientific or empirical investigation, and go 'beyond' what we can know, that is, 'the territory of pure understanding'. But they also cannot be within the scope of synthetic *a priori* knowledge. These ideas (of reason) cannot be the subject of synthetic judgements, since the latter require the human impositions of space and time, and God has to be beyond space and time, if not a human construct. Since such ideas are not amenable to either empirical or synthetic *a priori* judgements, they must lie outside the boundaries of knowledge altogether. That is, they lie outside the scope of all theoretical (scientific) reasoning.

Now, an empiricist who was faced with this situation would have to conclude that all talk of such ideas as God, freedom and immortality would be meaningless babble. If the only kind of reasoning is scientific or theoretical, and if these ideas lie outside the scope of such reasoning, then all talk of them would be un-reasoned. And this unhappy conclusion would have to be Kant's, too, were it not for his theory of transcendental idealism. That theory gives Kant the hope of concluding otherwise.

If theoretical reason were all that there is, then Kant would have to accept this conclusion. But transcendental idealism gives us a possible way out. For, according to transcendental idealism, speaking of things theoretically, that is, as objects of knowledge (phenomena), is not the only way of speaking of them. From another point of view, we may speak of them as things in themselves (noumena), that is, non-theoretically and independent of the conditions of knowledge. And such talk might still be reasonable; it is just not an exercising of theoretical reason. But if reason has another mode than the theoretical (where we are concerned to state claims of knowledge), what is it? Kant's answer is that reason may also be practical.

We humans are not just concerned to speak scientifically, and so to make verifiable knowledge claims. We are also agents, and as such are concerned to express genuine presuppositions of our practical activity. In particular, as agents, we must presuppose our own freedom. Kant's hope is that through the use of practical reason, we may legitimately speak not only of freedom, but of God, immortality, morality and even, beauty. This, in outline, is how Kant proposes to defend the possibility of theology, morality and aesthetics from the fact that they do not fit into science. They may still be rational, even though inaccessible to scientific reason. To defend the possibility of these disciplines might be seen as the underlying purpose of the *Critique of Pure Reason*. How Kant explores the legitimacy of morality and theology will be the subject of subsequent chapters. But let us illustrate his method by briefly considering his treatment of freedom.[12]

When one considers the occurrences in the world scientifically, from the point of view of theoretical reason, we cannot help but see them in terms of causal laws. Causation is a precondition of the theoretical standpoint. In fact, Kant thinks that strict causal determinism is a precondition of science. This is true for all occurrences, not just impersonal occurrences like thunderstorms but human actions, too. There are phenomenal occurrences too, amenable to scientific investigations, and as such, as fully governed by the laws of strict causal determinism as any others.

Take Kant's example of a malicious lie, voluntarily told by someone to cause great confusion in society. This is fully causally determined, if we look for the causes in the agent's bad upbringing, or perhaps, in his neuro-physiological brain state. But in spite of this scientific causal account of his action, we nevertheless find ourselves deeply committed to blaming the agent for the malicious lie. But to do this is to ascribe to the subject free will upon which morality depends. Now, on a non-Kantian philosophical theory, to ascribe to this agent both freedom and complete subjection to the strict causal laws of science would appear to be a straightforward contradiction; and Kant calls this situation an antinomy. However, transcendental idealism gives us the hope of escaping from the contradiction.

For transcendental idealism, there is not just one way that reason may function. Reason functions in terms of both empirical and moral action; it is applied to things (physical objects) and to thinking 'for oneself' (autonomous action). From the theoretical standpoint, we regard empirical action as causally determined. But, as will be discussed further in the next chapter, from the point of view of practical reason, we treat moral action as free and autonomous. There are not just phenomena, but there are also noumena. According to transcendental idealism, what we say about the agent from these two points of view cannot contradict each other, since utterances made from the two standpoints are subject to radically different concerns. From the theoretical standpoint, we search for the occurrences temporally prior efficient cause. From the practical standpoint, we treat the action as purposive; that is, as being performed by the agent freely for a reason; and when 'moral', this reason must be for 'the sake of duty alone'.[13]

How well Kant's theory of freedom works is the subject of much dispute. But it rests on making a sharp division between appearances and things-in-themselves; this means things regarded from the point of view of knowledge and things regarded from the point of view of practical agency. Crucially, according to Kant, ascribing freedom to an agent is something completely outside the realms of knowledge. But recall from an earlier quotation, which we repeat here, that Kant adds,

> though I cannot *know*, I can yet *think* freedom; that is to say, the representation of it is at least not self-contradictory, provided due account be taken of our critical distinction between the two modes of representation, that sensible and the intellectual, and the resulting limitation of the pure concepts of understanding and of the principles which flow from them.[14]

He has not established our freedom as a matter of scientific fact. Rather, more modestly, he has shown that the possibility of a non-scientific standpoint renders the ascription of freedom to oneself at least not self-contradictory. This is a difficult lesson for us to learn, for it is a feature of us as humans that our theoretical reason tries to get above itself and to attempt to draw conclusions about things which are outside its domain. It tries to speculate about such ideas as freedom and God as though they were possible objects of scientific knowledge. But the tendency is one to be resisted.

In this chapter, we have outlined the overall framework which allows Kant to make room for the possibility of morality and theology. Neither of these disciplines can be undermined by science, since they are inherently non-scientific. But this is by no means to render them unreasonable and matters of idle speculation. On the contrary, they are rational; it is just that they are matters of practical reason and not of theoretical reason. The nature of practical reasoning, that is, moral reasoning into which Kant aims to locate theology will be explored in the next chapter.

Chapter 2
'Moral Religion' for Theologians[1]

Kant's Morality: The Second *Critique* and the *Groundwork*

The moral law is holy *(inviolable). A human being is indeed unholy enough but the* humanity *in his person must be holy to him. In the whole of creation everything one wants and over which one has any power can also be used* merely as a means; *a human being alone, and with him every rational creature, is* an *end in itself; by virtue of the autonomy of his freedom he is the subject of the moral law, which is holy.[2]*

[W]hen we think of ourselves as free we transfer ourselves into the world of understanding as members of it and cognize autonomy of the will along with its consequence, morality; but if we think of ourselves as put under obligation we regard ourselves as belonging to the world of sense and yet at the same time to the world of understanding.[3] . . .

. . . what, then, can freedom of the will be other than autonomy, that is, the will's property of being a law to itself? But the proposition, the will is in all its actions a law to itself, indicates only the principle, to act on no other maxim than that which can also have as object itself as a universal law. This, however, is precisely the formula of the categorical imperative and is the principle of morality.[4]

There is no point in trying to dispute the fact that Kant's morality becomes 'moral religion'. Yet we might want to debate the different interpretations of his conception of moral religion. To do so, we need to consider closely the nature of Kant's morality, first of all; and our proposal here is to consider morality in the terms of Kant's transcendental idealism, focusing on how these terms shape human freedom, as it was introduced in the previous chapter. Now, it will remain crucial for Kant's conception of what binds us to together in 'religion' (that is, 'within the boundaries of mere reason') that, according to transcendental idealism, reason in its theoretical capacity cannot know anything beyond space and time, while within space and time our natural inclinations are determined by causal laws; at the very same time, in its practical capacity, reason enables (moral) agents to think for themselves, and to act – in Kant's terms – 'for the sake of duty alone'.[5] This last phrase captures what it is for Kant to act rationally and morally: it is to be free to do 'what one ought to do'. The specifics of this moral 'ought' are worked out, in different formulations of Kant's famous 'categorical imperative', essentially compatible with: 'act only' on a 'maxim' that could become a 'universal law'.[6]

For Kant, it is the universality of 'mere reason' that makes religion moral and morality religious: rationality binds human beings together in respect for each other and for the good represented by 'the moral law' – a central, technical conception in Kant's morality – to which we will turn in this and later chapters. The crucial point for 'moral religion' as understood in the present chapter is that we respect what is holy, and this is the humanity in us; and, as we will demonstrate here, for Kant this humanity in us is our rationality. Of course, it takes a considerable amount of reflection on Kant's writings before we begin to grasp what more exactly he means by 'rationality'. For the moment it is enough to know it is bound up with Kant's conceptions of freedom, morality, autonomy and what makes humanity holy in-itself.

Contemporary theologians, especially philosophers of the Christian religion, debate whether Kant is a 'moral theist', a 'deist', or even, an 'atheist'; that is, a great gap exists between those who read Kant as requiring a personal, good God for morality and as rejecting a personal, Creator God, or even, any God at all.[7] These are fascinating questions for philosophical theologians or Christian philosophers of religion, in particular. However, for the purposes of our argument here, in *Kant and Theology*, about Kant's two-aspect account of freedom, reason and religion, we will simply accept that Kant's morality, like his metaphysics, is deeply shaped by his Protestant Christian view of humanity; and then, we will aim to demonstrate the significance of Kant's moral religion for contemporary theology, but also for anyone aiming to read Kant's moral and religious philosophy.

Kant's moral religion is not only shaped in reaction to the 'enthusiasm' of his Pietistic upbringing,[8] but by a deeply held belief in human nature as distinct from both other animals and the rest of physical nature: what makes for the distinctiveness of humanity is rationality. This belief in humanity binds us together – that is, in a religion – as rational, and so moral. In turn, this distinctiveness sets humanity apart – as holy[9] – that is, we can reason as humans in a manner which renders us different from the rest of sensible nature. And yet human subjects are never fully rational and so, even the 'holy one' himself, that is, the man Christ, would have to be 'compared with our ideal of moral perfection', or essentially with the moral law, in order for us to recognize his perfect goodness. In Kant's words,

> Nor could one give worse advice to morality than by
> wanting to derive it from examples. For, every example
> of it represented to me must itself first be appraised in
> accordance with principles of morality, as to whether it
> is also worthy to serve as an original example, that is, as
> a model; it can by no means authoritatively provide
> the concept of morality. Even the Holy One of the

Gospel must first be compared with our ideal of moral perfection before he is cognized as such.[10]

Furthermore, implied above is Kant's rejection of 'a divine command theory'. Kant rejects the premise that the good comes from (what at least he calls 'slave-ish') following of God's commands as stipulating good. Instead even 'God' – as above, in Christ, the holy man – must be measured against an independent standard of the good, that is, the universal moral law of human reason.

As seen in the previous chapter, Kant's first *Critique* demonstrates that although the natural world is (and so, phenomena are) determined by causal laws, human beings are free insofar as they act rationally. So, we share rationality, that is, the distinctive feature of moral religion, as humans. This allows us not only to be bound together in a moral religion, but to be freed from the determinations of nature, or 'the sensible world'. In his *Groundwork of the Metaphysics of Morals*, Kant returns to his language about 'two worlds': the 'sensible' and the 'intelligible', or 'the world of sense' and 'the world of understanding'.[11] In both his *Groundwork* and his *Critique of Practical Reason*, Kant recounts how practical reasoning, or simply 'rationality', 'transports' us into an 'intelligible order', or 'world of understanding' while at the same time we still act in the 'sensible world' or 'world of sense';[12] that is, we act in the world of appearances, in space and time, and so are determined by natural laws. Similarly, actions determined by natural inclinations, by unruly desires or by anything which makes up our physical bodies will be non-moral or immoral. And yet it is possible to try to distance Kant from a literal reading of the 'two-worlds' and opt, instead, for accepting an inevitable – but not necessarily debilitating – tension between viewing (moral) action from two standpoints, or aspects: one sensible and the other intelligible; similarly, according to the rational and to the non-rational or irrational thinking.

In *Kant and Theology*, we are proposing that when such distinctions are expressed in 'two-worlds' language, it is best to interpret them metaphorically, and not read literally as two separate 'worlds'. This 'best' interpretation is made on philosophical grounds: we can make philosophical sense of the 'worlds' in Kant's transcendental idealist claims about rationality and practical reasoning as two-ways in which we can view human subjects and their actions. This means that Kant's transcendental idealism can make sense of his compatibilist view of free will and determinism. Roughly, this means that human subjects are sensible and determined by natural inclinations; and yet they can act morally, that is, rationally, as long as they are viewed not merely from the standpoint of nature and its causal laws; that is, human agents are two-aspect subjects. A subject is moral and rational when she acts according to the universal law of humanity, but her natural inclinations are still determined in acting in time and space, that is, in an individual body. Bodies individuate; and each of us is an embodiment of reason; so, what we share is 'the moral law within'[13] our nature as rational beings. What makes us free is the law, insofar as we are acting for the sake of that which we give to ourselves, that is, autonomously. To be determined merely by our sensible nature, and so, our many disparate desires renders us heteronomous; this, for Kant, would make us un-free.

In addition, Kant's two-aspect interpretation of human freedom and nature enables us to understand how it is that morality, for Kant, always remains an 'ought'. Actions are moral because we do what we 'ought' and not follow what 'is' our inclination. So, despite reason and inclination being in a tension, we can quite happily describe the 'is' of our sensible nature, while asking of morality whether we have done what we ought to do, and so acted rationally. Thus, there are always two aspects to Kant's moral religion: the 'is' of description and the 'ought' of prescription. Furthermore, the latter focuses upon the maxim of our action. Kant stipulates that a maxim is 'the subjective underlying principle' of any action; a moral agent will ask whether her maxim could become a universal law; if so, it is a good maxim, and acting on this maxim would be moral. Our moral religion brings human moral subjects together in a 'king-dom' in which we each aim to act for the sake of duty alone; the ideal is a kingdom of ends. What gives us the motivation to act as we ought is the hope that our autonomous actions will be rewarded with happiness compatible with virtue. But here I'm running ahead of my argument in anticipation of Kant's ideals of pure reason, and so his transcendent metaphysic which links the transcendental dialectic in the *Critique of Pure Reason* with *Religion within the Boundaries of Mere Reason*.

In his *Groundwork of Metaphysics of Moral*, Kant demonstrates how it is he came upon the idea that the universal law of rational human agents is holy, making us more than animals determined to act by our natural inclinations. Moreover, in the process, he develops four different possible formulations of the universal law as a categorical imperative;[14] that is, as a com-mand which is unconditional for all moral beings. To be moral is to act for duty alone; acting for the sake of duty alone means treating oneself and every other rational being as an end in herself and never merely as a means. Again, the maxim of an action which treats others and oneself as an end in themselves would be a good maxim; and acting on this maxim would be moral. Rationality requires that we respect each other and act consistent with our respect for each other – each – as an instance of the moral law. Of course, humans in not being fully rational are not perfectly good and so, they/we fail to act as they/we ought. Thus we know that we are not holy. Nevertheless that which is in us and distinguishes us as human remains holy.

Philosophers and theologians alike have in the history of Western ethics, and in moral theology, found Kant's morality highly demanding – often rejecting it as too demanding. But it might also be thought that his sense of duty and high regard for human dignity as a respect for our rational nature reflects a certain Christian distinction between things of 'this world' and a 'higher' world; the latter being 'spiritual', the former being 'worldly', or 'earthly' in a lesser or pejorative sense.

Nevertheless, it is undeniable from his philosophical writings that Kant does not hold to a strong view of human depravity or sin; the latter certainly does not damage human reason which we share, so that our reasoning cannot be trusted. Nor does, or can, Kant deny our embodiment as humans and finite: we cannot be divine, but nor can we know, or 'experience', as human without bodies in space and time. Instead Kant sees the moral law in us (humans) as holy; and rationality is the means to control our necessary, however contingent and natural inclinations, including unruly desires or heteronomous motivations. In this light, Kant's anthropology is close to orthodox Christian theology, but the critical nuances of his philosophical distinctions must be kept in mind.

So, why do Christian theologians, and especially much of contemporary Christian moral theology, reject Kant's moral religion? Often treating Kant as an enemy of Christianity? An atheist, or something worse, for example, someone who is spiritually or emotionally damaging to human relationships and so religious life itself? These questions are rhetorical at least at this stage, since it is more useful to turn to Kant's theological contribution to debates about Christ at this point. Christ will serve as an 'archetype', or 'prototype'.[15] Christ's two natures, even if unwittingly, create the significant possibilities for grasping Kant's conception of 'the good moral disposition'. One possibility is that the human (autonomous) agent as a two-aspect subject is ideally represented by Christ, that is, as the holy one incarnated – born in a human body – in space and time. We might say (symbolically) that, for Kant, Christ represents a self-temporalizing, and a spatialization of God as a perfect moral agent.

Ironically, though, it must be readily acknowledged that the strongest ground for theologians to read Kant, that is, his moral religion premised upon his high view of humanity as holy insofar as rational, is also the strongest obstacle for theologians who believe that humans are 'fallen', especially depraved not only in their sensible nature, but in their intelligible aspect; for these Christian critics, the latter is bound up with immorality in the sense of selfishness and pride. Crudely put, 'autonomy' in Kant has been read by certain theologians as 'self-centredness', or even selfishness; hope in achieving virtue through autonomous action worthy of happiness as sinful pride, or hubris. So, moral condemnation of Kant by twentieth-century theologians has focused on precisely where Kant insists humanity is bound together in a holy alliance.[16]

Allen W. Wood captures this ironic situation with clarity and unnanced condemnation. To quote a few lines from Wood:

> Much of popular religion now sees itself as 'correcting' the 'one-sidedness' of modern Enlightenment culture by privileging what is irrational and parochial, defending tradition, authority and superstition. It would reject such descriptions, of course, for it pays fervent lip service to spiritual freedom, even to the point of treating rational doubt and secular culture as sinister forces attempting to encroach on that freedom. But the 'religious freedom' it seeks to protect has little in common with Enlightenment spirit of thinking (rationally, universally) for oneself – a spirit that courageously accepts the anxiety, instability, discontent and self-alienation that rational thinking inevitably brings with it.[17]

Nevertheless, Kant and his moral philosophy stand firm, insofar as we reason autonomously we share the moral law and standard for the kingdom of ends – that is, they are united by autonomy in the universal law of our nature as rational and human, or what Kant also calls, 'the kingdom of God'.[18] The kingdom of God as a symbol is associated with the prototype (that is, Christ) of the good moral disposition. Together they serve as schemata in temporalizing the non-temporal aspect of Kant's moral religion.

In this light, why should either religion or theology today maintain a bias against Kantian rationality and autonomy? Our answer to this question should be clear by the time we reach the Conclusion of the present book, we will hope to have demonstrated our view that any theological rejection of Kant on the mere grounds of 'rationality' or 'autonomy' will surely have missed something significant in his 'moral religion', not least, equivocating on the use of these concepts by trying to be moral (and religious) without them. For one thing, it should already be clear that Kant is misunderstood when his philo-sophical contribution is reduced to scientific or psychological reasoning. For another, Kant has a great deal to say about moral-ity, thinking for oneself and the relations between human and divine. Perhaps most significant here is his possible contribution to theological discussions of Christ, sin and salvation; in par-ticular, Kant's moral religion brings about the schematization of Christ's nature as the 'archetype' of, what we would call, Kant's 'two-aspect subject'.

The archetype of Christ is not schematized as a 'moral guide', as much as it serves as the figure enabling us to make sense of why Kant finds it necessary to postulate his three ideals of reason: that is, freedom, immortality and the existence of God. We will return to Christ and the theological implications of the archetype of the good moral disposition in Chapter 4 and in our concluding remarks. But at this point, let us work to assess critically Kant's distinctions and connections between practical reasoning, freedom and autonomy.

Practical Reasoning, Freedom and Autonomy: Critical Distinctions

In focusing on Kant's *Critique of Practical Reason*, it is impossible here to rehearse all of the details in either Kant's analytic or dialectic of the concepts of pure practical reason.[19] However, we can focus upon a particular, salient example, in order to open up various questions concerning human freedom, reason, inclination, duty and autonomy. This opening is meant as a space for reflection on and through interpretation(s) of Kant.

One principle to bear in mind is that Kant, in his first *Critique*, radically limits the character of our self-knowledge. For example, Kant himself articulates this powerfully in the following footnote from the first *Critique*:

> The real morality of actions, their merit or guilt, even that of our own conduct, thus remains entirely hidden from us. Our imputations can refer only to the empirical character. How much of this character is ascribable to the pure effect of freedom, how much to mere nature, that is, to faults of temperament for which there is no responsibility, or to its happy constitution (*merito fortunae*), can never be determined; and upon it therefore no perfectly just judgements can be passed.[20]

Now, this limitation of self-knowledge – that is, 'real morality', and not the empirical character alone – necessitates an interpretation of the morality of actions – indirectly – by way of the social context of the (autonomous) agent, including the texts, the ritual practices and any other things which might reflect our moral and religious striving to be fully rational; in other words, to be holy, even if we know we cannot achieve this goal as long as we are human. It is helpful to interpret Kant's rational striving as similar to what philosophers who are appropriating Spinoza describe as 'our effort and desire to be', including the loss of the power to suffer; that is, a 'disability' which remains more profound and so hidden than the loss of an ability to act.[21]

Aiming for a better understanding of our freedom, rationality and morality, we propose to scrutinize one example from Kant, in relation to our contemporary cultural contexts. We intend to illustrate the sense in which Kant's moral law – that is, that we ought to act for the sake of duty alone – is a 'fact of pure reason'.[22] Consider carefully the following:

> Suppose someone asserts his lustful inclination that,
> when the desired object and the opportunity are present,

it is quite irresistible to him; ask him whether, if a gallows were erected in front of the house where he finds this opportunity and he would be hanged on it immediately after gratifying his lust, he would not then control his inclination. One need not conjecture very long what he would reply. But ask him whether, if his prince demanded, on pain of the same immediate execution, that he give false testimony against an honorable man whom the prince would like to destroy under a plausible pretext, he would consider it possible to overcome his love of life, however great it may be. He would perhaps not venture to assert whether he would do it or not, but he must admit without hesitation that it would be possible for him. He judges, therefore, that he can do something because he is aware that he ought to do it and cognizes freedom within him, which, without the moral law, would have remained unknown to him.[23]

The above aims to demonstrate, first of all, that in Kantian terms human beings possess a consciousness of the moral law as the self-legislation which links freedom and law. Each technical term, that is, duty, pure reason, moral law, self-legislation and freedom, has to be understood within the context of Kant's critical philosophy. Although his second *Critique* – is a text in moral philosophy, it continues a line of thinking already begun in the first *Critique*. In the latter, as we have already seen, Kant has established that there is no inconsistency in holding the idea of transcendental freedom, along with the causal structure of the empirical world of nature; yet with pure theoretical reason alone, Kant was not able to demonstrate the full reality of human freedom. So, practical reason is necessary to recognize that the moral law 'proves not only the possibility but the reality [of freedom] in beings who cognize this law as binding upon them'.[24]

In addition to illustrating the fact that we have a consciousness of the moral law our example demonstrates, second, that

Kant describes two possible cases of a subject's choice of action. The question is which subject acts *autonomously*? To answer, we can explore the ways in which the person who faces these choices is a highly specific two-aspect subject, as well as explore the two aspects inherent in Kant's principles of theoretical and practical reason.

For one thing, the subject is specific because he *(sic)* seems to be a man of the eighteenth century with all of the specifics of his sensible nature in a physical body. So, he is not a timeless, gender-neutral figure as tends to be assumed in the readings of Kant's text by certain Anglo-American analytic philosophers. The subject in Kant's examples generally reflects his own eighteenth-century assumptions about lust as a contingent and heavily value-laden desire. This becomes especially revealing *if* we suppose the reference to lust as an instance of sexual desire.

Consider a slight detour (from our example) via Kant's *Lectures on Ethics*. Here Kant assumes that lust is always for an object. He reasons that if the lust is for sex, then the object, whether a female subject or not, cannot be treated as a rational human being. This treatment of a subject as an empirical object is determined by the assumptions concerning the nature of sexual desire. Sexual desire always creates a situation in which the other is objectified.[25] In this context, sexual desire treats its object as a means to its satisfaction and not as a human being, that is, not as a subject with intrinsic value as such. In his *Lectures on Ethics*, the discussion of sexual desire clearly assumes heterosexual lust, that is, that of a man for a woman who is the object of his lust. But, arguably, the implicit problem with lust as the objectification of the desired 'subject' as an 'object' would be the same in homosexual desire.

Let us assume that in Kant's example of sexual desire the cultural differences more generally relevant to his account of lust could be part of twenty-first-century discussions of the central example from the second *Critique*. For instance, not everyone today would think of lust as a sin; and there are open debates about whether objectification is a necessary part of sexual desire or not.[26] For an additional cultural difference, consider the ways in which the subject of our example reflects eighteenth-century assumptions about moral maxims: here 'mutually good' describes the moral view of honour and truth-telling in 1785. A man should see it as a duty to tell the truth and defend another man's honour. By contrast, at the beginning of the twenty-first century, neither telling the truth nor defending another's honour is necessarily (in fact, rarely) a moral obligation that should be kept at the threat of death.

For another thing, concerning our subject (agent) who is presented with two very different choices, he is located in a highly specific context by Kant's assumed correlation drawn between the two cases of lust and false testimony. These two cases do not seem to correlate according to any obvious, twenty-first-century standards at least. The correlation is not based upon any apparent logic, analogy or present-day moral code. When pushed, a twenty-first-century reader might well wonder what it is that renders any correlation between Kant's cases. For us, his correlation begins to work insofar as we come to understand Kant's own assumptions about duty, as well as his assumptions about the maxim which guides an action. Kant defines a maxim, to repeat, as a subjective underlying principle of an action such as the moral maxim: refrain from false testimony.

Now, to facilitate our interpretation of this example (and this is definitely not meant to be the only possible interpretation of it), let us raise a critical question that continues to plague readers of Kant's texts: can a Kantian subject freely do a morally wrong action? Or, for Kant, is the determination of an immoral action *necessitated* by sensuous nature? The interpretative task of the theologian who follows Kant would be to understand the text, in order to achieve what he calls, in his third *Critique the Power of Judgment,* 'a broad-minded way of thinking'; this thinking intends to expand the conscious horizons of the readers.[27] Here Kant's principle of 'broad-minded thought' is to think 'in the position of everyone else'. As one of Kant's maxims of autonomous thinking found in Kant's third *Critique* this maxim is 'the power of judgment'.[28] We apply this principle to our example of Kant's practical reasoning, in order to make clear the issues surrounding the two central cases.

In the first case, the man is about to act in response to his lustful inclination for a desired object. It is most revealing for our interpretation of the theological meaning of Kant's text when we take lust – which is left unspecified in our example – as sexual desire. We might call sexual desire a distinctive case of lust; but bear in mind, lust is in any case difficult to read in terms of the earlier reference to the 'real morality of action'. The desired object could be a woman or another man in the house where he finds the opportunity to gratify his lust (even if we don't know the real morality of this act of desire).[29]

To understand better the background on sexual desire in Kant's *Lectures on Ethics*[30] consider this passage:

The desire which a man has for a woman is not directed towards her because she is a woman; that she is a human being is of no concern to the man; only her sex is the object of his desires. Human nature is thus subordinated. Hence it comes that all men and women do their best to make not their human nature but their sex more alluring and direct their activities and lusts entirely towards sex. Human nature is thereby sacrificed to sex. If then a man wishes to satisfy his desire, and woman hers, they stimulate each other's desire; their inclinations meet, but their object is not human nature but sex, and each of them dishonours the human nature of the other.[31]

So when we consider, in Kant's terms, whether the man in our central example (whose object of lust is not fully described) would gratify his sexual lust or not, we should realize that this gratification would mean denial of human nature. And this denial would mean that the gratification cannot be moral. If the man knows that this action of gratifying his lust would lead immediately to his own execution, he then discovers, perhaps unwittingly, the possibility to act otherwise. Kant suggests that when the alternative action would preserve his life, it is *un*likely the man would act out of lust. [Note that Kant does not seem to suggest that self-preservation is a duty, but that it is a stronger inclination than lust; and this seems to be the correct interpretation once we look at the second choice in which self-preservation is opposed to action for the sake of duty.] Some commentators have read the maxim of the action to preserve oneself as determined by a sensuous or natural inclination. Alternatively, this action is freely chosen, so not determined, yet still not a duty, since a result of non-moral inclination. Here we return to the huge, unresolved question as to whether or not a human subject can freely do an immoral action.

In the second case, it is necessary to imagine that the man, under the same threat of execution, is asked to give false testimony against an honourable man. Here we recognize not only the man's freedom of choice, but that he is free to act for the sake of duty, despite the fact that this will lead to his immediate execution.

In both cases the man is inclined to an action; but the inclination to gratify lust and the inclination to lie are both non-moral, if not, immoral. Acting freely *and* morally – hence, autonomously – can only be for Kant an action done for the sake of duty. In an answer to the persistent question, can the subject act freely and immorally? We are to agree that, for Kant, in the first case the action could be freely performed but not according to a moral maxim: whether non-moral or immoral both lust and self-preservation are either determined by, or result from a choice to follow, natural inclinations. To resolve ambiguity, at least somewhat, we maintain a distinction between freedom and autonomy: non-moral or immoral maxims can be freely, but not autonomously, chosen. If the man had followed his lust, despite the threat of execution, this would not be for Kant an autonomous act, since whether free or not it is done according to inclinations (and not for the sake of duty alone). In contrast, choosing to preserve one's life would be to act freely and autonomously against one's lustful inclinations. Yet the second case illustrates that self-preservation is *not* a duty, since merely fulfilling a natural inclination. Thus Kant intends to demonstrate that the subject chooses to act autonomously – that is freely *and* morally – only when he acts for the sake of duty, overriding any inclination for self-preservation. Ultimately, it remains a question for interpretation, whether the maxim of this moral action is the duty to always act for the sake of another man's honour. Or, is it for the sake of the duty to refrain from false testimony?

The general point of this example from the second *Critique* is that: no matter what the man chooses to do, he recognizes the freedom to make a moral choice in acting for the sake of duty rather than either following natural inclinations or choosing to follow an immoral maxim. But a further point of interpretation should be made about the difference between the two cases. That is, although a point of contention for Kantian formalists and their critics, the particular context of an action is necessarily involved in Kant's moral religion. Particularities are involved in the Kantian picture, since present in deciding which maxim should guide an action. It is these particularities of the context (of interpretation) that also make us vulnerable.

To support this claim, we refer our readers to Onora O'Neill's account of the power of examples in Kant. O'Neill argues for a dimension of 'particularism' in Kant's thinking, rejecting a sharp opposition between a focus on the universal law in Kant and the particulars of a concrete case.[32] More significant than examples, or any empirical claims, is the ability to reason practically. The important thing in Kantian reasoning is to know how to apply moral, yet always revisable, interpretations of principles. In a later context, O'Neill herself advocates 'a principled autonomy' in her reading of Kant.[33] Yet here a concern with the particulars of working out a maxim for action is crucial for the response given to those theological and philosophical critics of Kant who deny that particularities come into his ethics.[34]

Our example from Kant is meant to demonstrate that the moral law provides reasons for action which are not determined by the content and strength of a person's desires alone. For Kant in the *Groundwork to the Metaphysics of Morals*, desires like inclinations are, or can be, determined by nature; but this is what raises the major critical question. Can these be chosen or not as the maxim of one's action? Practical reason may require 'the man' to set aside or override desire-based reasons. If our focus was on the concept of desire, we might question a supposed independence of reason from desire. Yet our example seeks to demonstrate that the ability to act from the moral law is the ability to do something simply because it is judged to be a duty; and that duty as an 'ought' reflects the tensions of reason and desire (as inclination). This ability to act autonomously, then, reveals the human capacity to do something free of determination by natural causality; but this is not to forget the particulars of the context or desires. The point of the example is to stress that 'the sole fact of reason' is the moral law by which we recognize the capacity to act freely in terms not of the 'matter' but the 'form' of the law: this would be autonomous action.[35] It should be remembered that this practical use of reason gives reality to an idea of freedom which reason in its pure theoretical use could assume as possible, but could not establish. Thus, Kant demonstrates the *primacy* of practical reason (at least, for human freedom).

Kant's example can also be used to demonstrate that the moral law is first, that is, prior to the idea of freedom. The moral law is able to establish the reality of human freedom and autonomy. Kant takes autonomy literally as self-law: it is the fact that the will is a law to itself; or that our actions are autonomous insofar as we act consistent with the law of our own rational nature; and this would be the moral law. In acting in this way, as embodied subjects we, then, act freely, morally *and* rationally. In other words, Kant's conception of autonomy is not simply independence, but acting as we ought to, as free, moral and rational. Kant's conception – contrary to certain recent philosophical accounts – allows for us to remain in very specific, often deeply problematic ways vulnerable to and dependent upon both other people and an evolving context.

To understand autonomy's place in practical reasoning it must be grasped in the context of Kant's texts. Yet we must also be able to think with his texts in order to engage critically with the role of his practical reasoning in ethical reflection. A contemporary theologian might at this point raise a theological concern which has increased in depth and magnitude, since the twentieth century; that is, 'our understanding of the nature of texts and how we use them' which we call 'hermeneutics'.[36] This understanding has been especially the focus of theologians who draw their knowledge of God from the Bible and so need to be good at understanding ancient and authoritative texts; but hermeneutics is not only used as a biblical tool. As David Jasper explains,

> Hermeneutics is not an everyday term but it is a useful technical term ...
> it is about the most fundamental ways in which we perceive the world, think and understand. It has a philosophical root in ... *epistemology* – ... the problem of ... how we think and legitimate the claims we make to know the truth.[37]

Now, the concepts which we have been reading in Kant's texts in metaphysics, moral and religious philosophy have become part of any ongoing philosophical history of interpretation, or a critical hermeneutics, again probably more familiar to theologians than to philosophers in the English-speaking world at least. Here 'critical' implies two hermeneutical moments: one of suspicion and the other of restoration of meaning.[38]

The hermeneuticist is meant to be a specialist both in being suspicious about what the text says and how we might be inclined to use it for our contemporary purposes; in seeking restoration, after this negative moment of suspicion of our hidden motives, there is a need to approach authoritative but distant texts in a new way, in order to restore critically their significance with greater understanding of our distance from the author's context and the potentially wider context of the text itself.

So, now, to complete the interpretation of our example, let us further reflect upon what is original in Kant's example for autonomous thinking, and how we might learn from this, for our final chapter on the critical reception of Kant on 'autonomy'. The second *Critique* contains this example of a subject who faces two sets of choices (i) to act according to either lust or self-preservation and (ii) to act according to either self-preservation or truth-telling. Presumably, the subject, or 'man' (*sic*), would act in the first case for self-preservation, and the rational man, or person, in the second case for both the sake of 'his' duty to tell the truth and to uphold the honour of another 'man'. But will this subject act in each case as an autonomous person? Autonomy seems only to come into the second choice; yet here we should consider thinking with Kant's concept.

This sort of thinking with philosophical concepts finds support from an unlikely context: a feminist appropriation of Hannah Arendt for a reading of the history of philosophy. The feminist philosopher Genevieve Lloyd claims that Arendt derives from Kant her 'engagement with the present', while 'thinking with' the concepts in the texts of a past philosopher. In particular, Lloyd stresses collaborative thinking: 'an exercise in remembering philosophical resources and extending them by putting them to new uses in response to circumstances which call them forth'.[39] In other words, disagreement about how to interpret the first choice in Kant's example can also reveal something about current thinking, in contrast to eighteenth-century thinking. Some women and men today would risk death to satisfy lust without thinking that this is non-moral, or immoral. Kant would not agree. Nevertheless, we can recognize the limits and the possibilities of thinking with this example in the light of the social and material positionings of the subject, and the underlying principles of autonomy, practical reason and moral law. Michèle Le Doeuff insists that male and female philosophers must never lose the freedom to read philosophical texts for themselves. This freedom, according to Le Doeuff, constitutes autonomous thinking as the very essence of philosophy.

Theologians will be used to raising questions about how to interpret texts, not least from their work on biblical hermeneutics. However, theologians can also gain from the feminist and other philosophical readings of Kant as a crucial figure in the history of moral theology: these readings force entrenched theological assumptions and biases to be questioned, often radically. Two of these theological biases are assumptions that (1) reason is to be mistrusted, since (naturally) driven by selfish and/or sinful motives and (2) autonomy is assumed to be the source of pride, and/or domination of nature and of woman and as such, destructive of the Christian community. Instead, our contention is that Kantian autonomy should become a virtue even for Christian women who have been exclusively associated with sensible nature. Both reason and autonomy are wrongly supposed by certain Christian theologians, especially those influenced by Barth if not Calvin; to be the 'cause' of broken communities, broken families, wrecked marriages and sexual immorality generally. To project onto Kant and his moral conceptions the source of this magnitude of immorality and perhaps even a greater range of sin, is not only foolish, but a serious block to learning from Kant's moral religion. Instead Kant's moral religion could transform the discipline of theology when it is not turned in on itself, but is forward-looking and active globally in advocating human freedom, autonomy, practical reason – and so, Kant's moral religion.

Chapter 3
Theoretical and Practical Arguments for Theism

The Concept and Existence of God

In the first section of this chapter, we aim to explain how Kant conceived of God and give a critical account of Kant's reaction to the traditional, speculative arguments for the existence of the theistic God. After this, the intention is to examine how Kant believes the concept of God ought to be employed from both a scientific point of view, and a moral point of view. Finally, we will assess whether, given Kant's general philosophical approach, he is warranted in even talking about God.

Kant is well-known for his destructive criticism of the three traditional arguments for the existence of God. Less well-known is his positive claim, in the first *Critique*, that 'God' is a concept which is natural to human reason. An idea is an object of human reason. Kant defines an 'ideal' to be an instance of an idea of reason which is taken to be an individual existent. Kant calls God 'a transcendental ideal', meaning that it is not derived from experience.[1]

In order to show how the concept of God arises, Kant invokes his principle of determinability:

According to this principle, of every two contradictorily opposed predicates only one can belong to a concept. . . . But every *thing*, as regards its possibility, is likewise subject to the principle of complete determination, according to which if all the possible predicates of things

be taken together with their contradictory opposites,
then one of each pair of contradictory opposites must
belong to it.[2]

So the concept of any thing is completely determined once we
have specified which of each pair of contradictory predicates
it satisfies.

Kant assumes that in a complete list of predicates, each of
the predicates has a contradictory – such as powerful and
non-powerful. For each positive predicate, there is a negative
predicate. Given Kant's principle of determinability, he declares
that the human mind is naturally led to consider a thing which
satisfies exactly all positive predicates. This possessor of all
possible positive predicates is the *ens realissimum*, a supremely
perfect being or 'God'.[3] Given the definition, the *ens realissimum*, is

the whole store of material from which all possible
predicates of things must be taken.[4]

It is the thing from which all other objects derive their existence. We do not just have the concept of this object; we posit
its existence. This makes God an ideal:

[N]othing is an object *for us*, unless it presupposes the
sum of all empirical reality as the condition of its
possibility.[5]

The objection here is that Kant has not satisfactorily showed
us how the concept of the *ens realissimum* is constructed. It is
the possessor of all positive predicates; but what are these
positive predicates? Mortal and immortal both seem to be
positive predicates, and yet no object can satisfy them both.
Immortal is not the same as non-mortal, since a stone is non-
mortal, but not immortal.

Another objection is that 'God' is the possessor of predicates
like omnipotent, benevolent, etc. but not predicates like fragile,

clumsy, etc. In order to define God we need a criterion to pick out predicates of the former type and not the latter type. Kant gives us no such criterion. Whatever ideal Kant has defined, it is not God as traditionally conceived.

The Speculative Proofs: A Critique of Pure Theoretical Reason

Now, let us examine Kant's attitude to the proofs of God's existence. Kant divides the arguments into the speculative and the practical. Arguments of the latter type contain an ethical premise; those of the former type do not. In the first *Critique*, Kant attacks the speculative arguments. In the second *Critique*, he puts forward his own practical proof. Kant divides the speculative arguments into types: (1) those which do not and (2) those which do use a factual or existent premise. The only instance of (1) is the ontological argument. Those of type (2) may be divided into (2a), those in which the existential premise is extremely abstract; for example, 'something contingent exists'; and (2b) those in which the existential premise is quite definite, it takes the form 'Nature exists and contains *these* particular features'. The cosmological or First Cause argument is of type (2a). The physico-theological argument, or argument from design, is of type (2b). Kant claims that these three arguments are the only speculative arguments for the existence of God. It is likely that the historical order of the origin of these arguments is (2b), (2a) and (1). However, Kant claims that the logical order of the arguments is exactly the opposite. The physico-theological argument depends logically upon the cosmological argument, which depends upon the ontological argument. We will examine Kant's claim later in this chapter.

Let us consider, first of all, the ontological argument, which attempts to define God's existence from a definition. God as the *ens realissimum* is defined, in part, as the 'being which is omnipotent, omniscient, benevolent, etc . . .' So, anyone who claims that God is not omnipotent is either using the term God in a non-standard way or is contradicting oneself. Now, in fact, God is defined in part as the 'being which is *existent*, omnipotent, omniscient, . . .'. So for the same reasons as before, anyone who claims that God is not existent is either using God in a non-standard way or is contradicting oneself. So, 'God is existent' *must* be true, by definition. Therefore, God, with all the properties which theologians ascribe to Him, exists.

Kant objects to this argument by claiming that existent does not have the right to be listed among the properties of God or of anything. Existent things are not of a kind. Existence is not a state or a quantity. Kant sums this up by saying that existent is not a real predicate or a determining predicate. Certainly, 'exists' does often behave in sentences like a predicate. But this only makes it a grammatical or logical predicate. Kant makes his position clearer in the following quote:

> Anything . . . can . . . serve as a logical predicate; the subject can even be predicated of itself . . . But a determining predicate is a predicate which is added to the concept of the subject and enlarges it . . . 'Being' is obviously not a real predicate; that is, it is not a concept of something which could be added to the concept of a thing.[6]

Yet Kant offers little justification for his claim that existent is not a real predicate. It is not obvious how to defend his distinction between real/determining predicates and grammatical/logical predicates, since it is not clear how to characterize predicates, other than as grammatical terms. It is true that many formal logical languages adopt the convention of treating 'exists' as a quantifier, rather than as a predicate, but this convention does not serve as an argument to prove that 'exists' is not a predicate. It remains a live possibility that 'I possess the property of existing' is correctly formulated.

However, any such rejection of Kant's claim does not imply that one must accept the validity of the ontological argument.

This may be seen as follows. Let us adopt a realist approach to possible worlds. To say that an object, x, exists is to say that x is in the actual world (not other possible worlds). So exists may be treated as a normal predicate. Now, we have the concept of a dragon; it possesses properties such as breathing fire, etc. Now, let us define dragon★ as possessing all the typical properties of a dragon, with the added property of existing. So part of the concept of a dragon★ is that it is in the actual world, rather than in any other possible world. But, (i) there are no instantiations of dragon★ in any non-actual world since exists is a component, and (ii) there are none in the actual world; that is, an empirically discovered fact. Therefore, there is no instantiation of dragon★ in any possible world. Therefore, dragon★ is inconsistent.

We run the same risk of inconsistency, if we chose to define God as being existent. The ontological argument only allows us to make the following weak conclusion: *Either* God exists in *this* world *or* the concept of God is inconsistent. We cannot rule out the latter possibility. So, the ontological argument fails, whether or not we accept Kant's reason for its failure or the one presented here.

Second, Kant formulates the cosmological or first cause argument as follows:

> If we admit something as existing . . . we must also admit that there is something which exists necessarily. For the contingent exists only under the condition of some other contingent existence as its cause, and from this again we must infer yet another cause, until we are brought to a cause which is not contingent, and which is therefore unconditionally necessary.[7]

Here God's necessary existence refers to causal necessity, that is, God exists but has no cause.

The obvious objection to this formulation of the first cause argument is why should we say 'until we are brought to a cause which is not contingent'? Why not say, 'and so on *ad infinitum*?'

There is no need to invoke a first cause. Kant's main objection, however, is that the cosmological argument relies on the onto-logical argument. The cosmological arguers have supposedly proven that there is a necessarily existent being. But this might not be God. Necessary existence is just one aspect of God. They need to assume the further premise that every necessary existent is an *ens realissimum* (or perfect being). This is the converse of the fundamental step of the ontological argument. But we have the following principle: 'If every S is P and there is at least one S and at most one P, then every P is S.' Given that there can only be one *ens realissimum*, we have that – Every *ens realissimum* is a necessary existent. So, Kant claims, the cosmological argument assumes the ontological argument.

But we object that if, in the cosmological argument, we mean by necessarily existent, exists but has no cause, not exists by definition, then there is an ambiguity. So, we cannot apply the above principle to demonstrate the dependence of the cosmological argument on the ontological argument. Also, the cosmological arguers might be content with limited con-clusion that there is a first cause and not claim to prove the existence of the *ens realissimum*. They might believe that the first cause is God, but admit that they have no proof of this claim. So, Kant's claim of dependence is misleading.

Third, Kant states the physico-theological argument or argument from design as follows:

(1) Everywhere there are clear signs that the world is
ordered in accordance with a determinate purpose . . .
(2) This purposive order is quite alien to the things
of the world, and only belongs to them contingently;
[it was designed] by an ordering rational principle
in conformity with underlying ideas. (3) There exists,
therefore, a sublime and wise cause (or more than
one) . . . (4) The unity of the cause may be inferred
from [the way that different parts of the world act
in harmony].[8]

Although it is not explicitly stated, the justification for the second step is on analogy with complicated human-made machines. Kant has great respect for the persuasive power of this argument, but rejects it. He notes that

> This argument can indeed lead us to the point of
> admiring the greatness, wisdom, power, etc. of the
> author of the world, but can take us no further.[9]

Perhaps because of this respect, Kant spends very little time actually refuting the argument itself, in the first *Critique*. He does point out, though, that it relies on the cosmological argument and the ontological argument. Certainly, we agree that if a defense of the design argument infers the existence of anything *more* than a designer of the world, like a creator or perfect being, then the other argument must be used. But as in the cosmological case, the arguers might be contented with a limited conclusion.

We have mentioned Kant's respect for the design argument. This respect arises because Kant finds that it is internally scientifically useful to view the world *as if* it were divinely ordered. Now, this leads us to consider how the concept of God should be used from the point of view of science. Kant's view is that ideals of reason, such as God, should not be regarded as things which actually exist. Rather they should be treated as hypotheses which play a useful role of systematizing scientific data. Kant states this by declaring that God and other ideals of reason should be employed like regulative principles and not constitutive ones. We will return to consider these ideals in the context of practical reasoning, that is, in a non-theoretical sense, further on.

At this stage, let us see how C. D. Broad presents the difference between constitutive and regulative principles. He demonstrates how both of two constitutive principles have appeal to us as 'rational beings'; and yet they seem to contradict each other. First, '[i]f anything exists, then *something* must exist in its own right. It cannot be that *everything* that exists derives its existence from something else'.[10] Broad identifies this as 'the principle at the back of the cosmological argument', and moves on to assert: (2) '[i]t is impossible that the existence of anything should be a necessary consequence of its mere nature or definition'.[11] He concludes that the latter principle is 'fatal' to the ontological argument, and to the conclusion of the cosmological argument. Kant's own way out of this is to insist that these principles should not be treated as rules about things, but instead as methodological rules for the guidance of reason.

For his part, Broad reformulates (1) as the following maxim:

> In all your researches, try to explain everything that you can by deduction from the minimum number of ultimate facts and ultimate laws. Never be contented with a plurality of isolated brute facts, but try to make natural science as nearly as deductive science as you can.[12]

He restates (2) as the following warning:

> Remember nevertheless, that this ideal is in principle quite unattainable. No empirical thing exists of intrinsic necessity and no empirical law is intrinsically necessary. If a necessarily existent being were possible at all, it would be something quite inconceivable to us. And if nature depended on this being for its existence, this relation of dependence would be something quite different from the causal dependence of one event in nature upon earlier events, which is all that we can understand.'[13]

When (1) and (2) are interpreted as regulative principles, there is no contradiction.

From a scientific point of view, then, Kant thinks that theology may be invoked as a systematizing hypothesis. It is interesting to consider whether, perhaps, it is possible to perform the same systematizing role by invoking non-religious theories, such as evolution. While we have dealt with Kant's account of God from a scientific point of view, Kant himself maintains that the most significant use of God is for morality. He aims to demonstrate that the existence of God is a necessary hypothesis, if we, as moral agents, are to avoid practical irrationality. Kant regards morality as yielding a rational *belief* (*Vernunftglaube*) in God,[14] rather than an abstract theoretical knowledge. Religion rests upon morality, rather than vice versa as is commonly supposed.

Kant's Moral Argument: Belief in Practical Reason

Kant's moral argument for the existence of God, stated in the *Critique of Practical Reason*, may be summarized briefly as follows.[15] The complete good ought to exist. Therefore, it is possible. Therefore, anything which is an essential condition of its existence must be actual. Its possibility is not guaranteed by ordinary facts and laws of nature. We cannot find in the natural world anything which guarantees that people get their just deserts. So we are entitled to postulate a being on whom nature depends. This being is not merely powerful but good. We call the being God.[16]

We may attack the details of the argument. However, there is a general objection. The argument does not imply 'that God exists'. It merely shows that 'belief in God' would be very desirable for a moral agent to have, in order for the agent to avoid a practical paradox.[17] Allen Wood here points out an analogy with Pascal's wager: Pascal, like Kant, does not show that God exists and that Christianity is true, but rather that 'belief in' God as the highest good is advantageous for us to have.[18]

Now, let us consider if Kant was consistent in his own philosophical approach to say that we could even conceive of God. The first objection may be stated as follows. Kant is often claimed to hold a brand of phenomenalism or at least to have a phenomenalist strand. Strawson claims that Kant holds a principle of significance, under which metaphysical concepts, such as God, are meaningless.[19] We counter by pointing out that if Kant held a principle of significance, then it is not a verifiability criterion, of the type held by logical positivists. Kant does not claim that terms for metaphysical objects are meaningless; rather we cannot claim to have any knowledge of such objects.

There is a second, more particular, objection. Part of the concept of 'God' is that He is the 'creator of the world as a whole'. Kant previously claimed, in the first Antinomy in the *Critique of Pure Reason*, that we have no conception of the world as a whole.[20] It follows that we have no concept of God. Yet it is possible to defend Kant here by rephrasing this property of God in an acceptable form. For example, we might say that God is the 'creator of all totality'. This property has an acceptable form, since 'totality' is one of Kant's twelve categories. This defends Kant against the charge of inconsistency.

Moreover, if we recall what was demonstrated in Chapters 1 and 2 (above). We can assert that God remains for Kant one of those ideals of reason which he calls transcendental – about which we cannot have any empirical or synthetic *a priori* knowledge. And yet we can have, on the basis of pure practical reason, 'belief in' God as the highest good; that is, belief in postulating a state of affairs in which all agents have achieved virtue, and happiness is distributed in accordance with virtue. Admittedly, when it comes to the idea of God, there is no empirical content or intuition for cognition. Yet a practical vindication of the ideal of God starts from experience of the moral law, and specifically our awareness of not being fully rational, and yet striving to be rational; God is necessary for this rational and moral striving towards the completion of virtue as worthy of happiness.

We have already seen how the awareness of the moral law comes into Kant's second *Critique* in the cases where a clear difference exists from acting consistent with our natural inclinations and acting for the sake of duty alone. But even with this awareness of the moral law, that is, of what we ought to do, we are aware of both our imperfections and our irrationality. In words which almost sound as though they have come from the *New Testament*, Kant would agree that 'we do not always act as we ought to do'; we simply fail to be rational; and the source of this failure is not an empirical matter. In the next chapter, we will consider how autonomy is corrupted, and a 'radical' evil will arise from an 'inscrutable' origin, subverting the good moral maxims of human actions for evil ones. But note that Kant will not have God take moral responsibility away from human agents: human freedom means that God cannot 'save' humanity by making us servile to his commands.

Conclusion: On the Proofs for Theists

Kant argues that God is not an object of knowledge. Yet taking God's existence as a mere hypothesis – an *as if* – could be useful for scientists; that is, those who try to systematize data about the world. God is also a useful concept for the moral agent's practical rationality. However, this does not *compel* moral agents to believe in God. Such agents might see no reason to make consistent the set of beliefs which they hold. Since Kant holds that God is not an object of knowledge, he is obliged to claim that no non-moral argument can prove God's existence.

We agree, with Kant, that the three traditional theoretical arguments for God's existence fail; however, this does *not* imply, as Kant might at first be supposed to suggest that there is no proof for the existence of God; the moral argument remains. Although Kant is right to reject the traditional theistic arguments, it is arguable that he does so for the wrong reasons: in particular, his claim that 'exists' is not a real or determining predicate might be questioned. There is also the outstanding question as to whether the physico-theological argument and the cosmological argument do rest logically upon the ontological argument.[21]

To end this section on a more positive note, let us return our proposed use of 'belief in' God for Kant's postulate of practical reason. This would be distinct from 'belief that' God exists; this latter is a proposition and justifiable by cognition, if it can be demonstrated that the proposition has empirical content; the former – belief in – is more like an assertion of a conviction on which we can act, reflect and imagine with confidence.

The distinction between 'belief in' and 'belief that' has been successfully and creatively employed by A. W. Moore.[22] Moore concludes that

> Belief in God, on this way of construing it, is to be characterized by what it enables us to do, not by its content.[23]

Moore also directs us to *Fallen Freedom* by George Michalson, who although much more pessimistic than Moore about God's existence, maintains that Kant's ultimate goal remains 'moral religion', and historical forms of religions will do as long as the goal of 'rational religion' remains supreme. In Michalson's words, '[B]elief in God and confidence in morality grow out of the same metaphysical soil.'[24] This is consistent with Kant's postulates that belief in God is like belief in rationality, it enables us to do virtuous acts, but it is not determined by its empirical content. In the next chapter we will follow this discussion with a look at the postulate of immortality, moving on to discuss corruption, or radical evil, Christ as a prototype in Kant and the possibility of salvation from wrong-doing or evil.

Chapter 4

Immortality, Corruption/ 'Radical Evil' and Salvation

Religion as Shared Rationality versus Religion as Service to God

Human freedom both allows and requires us to strive for immortality as central to Kant's conception of moral religion. This will be demonstrated here by elucidating moral religion's relations to (1) immortality and rationality, (2) corruption/ 'radical evil' and freedom and (3) salvation and striving for the highest good. Before turning to the question of autonomy in its relation to corruption, let us recall what has been established concerning moral religion.

To begin with, consider the contrast of Kant's conception of religion as being bound together rationally to 'religion' conceived as 'cult', or religious 'service to God'. In Chapter 2, we found Kant arguing for moral religion with a case against religion as being gathered together, for example, in prayer.[1] Kant's 'religion' implies essentially human beings are already bound together by a shared rationality; and this conception required arguing against 'a religion of divine service'. Kant's own contrast, in the *Religion*, is as follows:

> If . . . we regard ourselves as duty-bound to behave not just as human beings but also as *citizens* within a divine state on earth, and to work for the existence of such an association under the name of a church, then the question How does God will to be honoured in *a church*

(as a congregation of God)? appears unanswerable by
mere reason, but to be in need of a statutory legislation
only proclaimed through revelation, hence of a historical
faith which we can call 'ecclesiastical' in contradistinction
to pure religious faith. For in pure religious faith it all
comes down to what constitutes the matter of the
veneration of God, namely, the observance in moral
disposition of all duties as his commands.[2] . . . However,
we should not . . . forthwith presume that the
determination of this form is a task of the divine
lawgiver; there is rather a reason to assume that it is
God's will that we should ourselves carry out the idea
of such a community.[3]

But it would be just as arrogant peremptorily to deny
that the way a church is organized may perhaps also be a
special divine dispensation, if, so far as we can see, the
church is in perfect harmony with moral religion, and if,
in addition, we cannot see how it could ever have
made its appearance all at once without the requisite
preparatory advances of the public in religious concepts.
Now, in hesitation over this task – whether God or
human beings themselves should found a church – there
is proof of the human propensity to a *religion of divine
service (cultus)*, and, since such a religion rests on arbitrary
precepts, to faith in statutory divine laws based on the
assumption that some divine legislation, not to be
discovered through reason but in need of revelation,
must supervene to even the best life conduct . . . attention
is thereby given to the veneration of the supreme being
directly (and not by way of that compliance to his
commands already prescribed to us through reason).
Thus it happens that human beings will never regard
either union into a church, or agreement over the form
to be given to it, or likewise any public institution for
the promotion of the moral [content] of religion, as
necessary in themselves but only for the purpose of, as

they say, serving their God, by means of festivities, professions of faith in revealed laws, and the observance of precepts that belong to the form of the church . . . Although all these observances are at bottom morally indifferent actions, yet, precisely for this reason, they are deemed to be all the more pleasing to God, since they are supposed to be carried out just for his sake.[4]

As already demonstrated in Chapter 2, for Kant, it is the universality of mere reason that makes religion moral and morality religious: rationality binds human beings towards in respect for each other and for the good represented by 'the moral law' as a technical conception in Kant's morality. The crucial point for moral religion is that we respect what is *holy*, and this is the humanity in us. For Kant, this humanity in us is our *rationality*. The decisive problem with 'the human propensity to *religion* . . . [as] *cultus*' (as in the long quotation above) is its arbitrariness, and not being 'religion' as shared rationally *as if* by divine commands.

Second, before turning to the question of corruption, or sin, in the form of Kant's conception of radical evil, and how Christ helps us to work out our own salvation, let us think more carefully about rationality both for life 'on earth' and life 'in heaven'. The latter life would imply immortality which is another one of Kant's ideals of reason, or postulates of practical reason.

Rationality and Immortality: Working towards Salvation by Way of Moral Certainty

If we introduce a notion of 'moral certainty' in Kant, we come close to belief in rationality as a form of 'pure religious faith'; and such 'belief in' serves as a translation of 'postulating' the existence of freedom, God and immortality.[5] At this stage, an example helps to illustrate how we come to believe in immortality.

So, let us recall the question of immortality. This is one of Kant's transcendental ideals about which we cannot have any empirical or synthetic *a priori* knowledge. In talking about the postulate of immortality as 'belief in' we do not have 'constitutive' knowledge. Yet some Kantian theologians today still argue with great energy (and cogency) that 'pure cognition' grounds 'Kant's'[6] Christian theology; their cognition of the idea of God is supported by reasoning which almost sounds like that of medieval theologians.[7] The critical question for theologians who think that they can 'cognize' ideas of immortality and God is, how can Kant's transcendental ideals have, or be, 'objects' of any sort of 'cognition', whether 'pure' cognition or not?[8]

Instead the view taken here in *Kant and Theology* is that 'what cannot be known' empirically or as synthetic *a priori* cannot be 'cognized'. So we cannot 'cognize' God, immortality or Christ as a prototype of moral goodness. But we do agree with Allen W. Wood's use of the language of 'regard as . . .' in the following:

> Kant denies that any theoretical cognition of God is required for religion . . . He infers from this that there need not be any special duties *to* God in order for there to be a religion . . . The duties we *regard as* divine commands are simply the duties we have as human beings to human beings.[9]

With no empirical content or intuition for cognition of God, it would not only push Kant too far to claim the ideals of God and immortality could be 'cognized' as 'ideas' in the mind. Instead we could not even know if God's commands are holy without the freedom to compare them, like any command, to the moral law for ourselves; that is, autonomously in Kant's sense.

Kant's practical vindication of the postulate of immortality, like that of God, is not intended to establish its truth – and so, we maintain, it is not cognized, whether by pure or empirical cognition. Certainly, to be fair, none of these theologians – in fact, no one – thinks that Kant claims cognition of God like empirical objects with truth-content. Instead Kant's practical vindication of immortality starts from our *moral* experience and specifically our awareness of not being fully rational; we are aware of both our imperfections and our irrationality. We do not always act as we ought to: we fail to be rational; and the source of this failure is not an empirical matter. But we stress more than this, Kant aims to demonstrate in the *Religion* that our irrationality – as evil – is 'radical' and 'inscrutable';[10] that is, radical evil like perfect (divine) goodness is beyond our comprehension; and yet this inscrutable reality is not superficial but profound and pervasive. It is crucially a practical reality, not theoretically cognizable.

At the same time, Kant still maintains that if we are to be virtuous it is up to us as rational agents to act for the sake of duty alone and aim to achieve virtue. So where does immortality come in? And can any divine assistance, or 'grace', help Kant? To answer the second question at least in part first of all.

It is clear that Kant always held, if you like, 'the conviction' that nothing ultimately results in our favour morally, except what results from our own virtuous endeavours. This is confirmed at the end of the *Religion* where Kant asserts:

> But thus far we cannot see how those who, in their
> opinion, have been exceptionally favoured (the elect)
> might in the slightest outdo the naturally honest human
> beings, who can be relied upon in daily affairs, in
> business and in need; on the contrary taken as a whole,
> they can hardly withstand comparison with him, which
> proves that the right way to advance is not from grace to
> virtue but rather from virtue to grace.[11]

In other words, salvation from Kant's 'radical evil', which is the corruption due to the subversion of our good 'maxims', (where maxims are the underlying subjective principles), of our moral action, is not a matter of grace from God. Instead, recall that Kant rests full responsibility on human agents for their wrongdoing. So Kant is certainly not advocating an orthodox Christian notion of divine grace, and certainly, no human (total) depravity. Nevertheless, we can say something very positive about Kant's philosophy of religion – and so, contribution to the theological discussions of corruption (or, 'sin') and human responsibility (so to speak, 'before God' understood as compatible with the highest good).

Basically, Kant insists upon human effort in all moral matters and this is a fundamental conviction. This use of conviction is different from a postulate, but it is linked to practical freedom which is a postulate and, also, a transcendental ideal. At the same time, Kant is equally aware that moral experience shows us how much our own change or 'reformation' depends upon the contingencies of life which are beyond our control. Another way of saying this latter point is that Kant's writings demonstrate that the possibility of our changing from evil to good maxims is out of our control.

Again, we think that A. W. Moore is very helpful in supporting the position which is taken in *Kant and Theology*. Moore creates an example which enables us to begin to grasp the moral certainty of immortality like – or, *as if* – belief in rationality.[12]

> To take a particularly crude but pertinent example,
> I cannot now initiate a process of reformation if I am
> about to have my life taken from me. So if we are to
> have any hope, we must assume that all the relevant
> contingencies obtain [for my life to continue].[13]

Moore develops this reasoning further, in order to demonstrate the nature of belief. Moore is close to Kant here, insofar as Kant's non-theoretical reasoning is not about truth or intuition, and it is not a 'lesser' form of empirical or synthetic *a priori* knowledge. Instead as Moore maintains, it can be read as a form of 'belief in'.[14] Moore clarifies this in the following nuanced response:

> . . . to pursue the example just considered, whether
> I am about to have my life taken from me makes no

difference to whether I ought, now, to respect the demands of reason. Certainly I ought.[15] But whether I *believe* that I am about to have my life taken from me does make a difference to whether I can keep that 'ought' properly in focus; whether, in the terms of the previous section, I can see it as suitably motivating and not just as a pointed reminder of all that I have failed to do and all that I have failed to be. To see the 'ought' as suitably motivating, I must think that there is still some point in respecting the demands of reason. To think that there is still some point in respecting the demands of reason, I must think that respecting them can be part of a new-found total commitment to doing what is right. To think this, I must think that the conditions of the possibility of making such a commitment, the conditions of the possibility of reforming, are satisfied. And to think that the conditions of the possibility of reforming are satisfied, I must think, not merely that I am not about to have my life taken from me, but, granted what was said in the previous section, that I enjoy *some* sort of immortality.[16]

Basically, in this light, Kant's practical vindication of 'the must' – as the requirement of – the postulate of immortality, like the postulates of God and of freedom, does not demonstrate their truth, or our knowledge of them. Instead it demonstrates the practical necessity that we believe in freedom, God and immortality, in order to sustain our hope and so our moral duty, to persevere in our rationality. Moore continues to support this hope and duty to persevere, while admitting the critical question it raises. Essentially, he illustrates a 'Kantian way' of dealing with conundrums:

To adopt a regulative ideal is to act *as if* some non-empirical idea has an application which we not only cannot know it has, but know it cannot have.

(The application which we hope the former has is beyond the bounds of our experience and knowledge: the application which we know the latter cannot have is within the bounds of our experience and knowledge.) But this difference also signals an equally fundamental similarity, which Kant himself notes. In each case we act as if some non-empirical idea has an application, though we cannot know it does.

In the former case, to repeat, we *hope* it does. And we must accordingly believe it does. This raises one of the most basic questions concerning the three postulates. In so far as we have no alternative but to believe them, can we take an ironic step back and concede that, even so, they may be false?' [17]

Moore argues that the answer is 'yes' and 'no'! Yes; we can recognize that our having no alternative except to believe in them does not entail their truth. No; we cannot convert that recognition into genuine agnosticism. If we really do have no alternative except to believe in them, then we have no alternative but to *believe* them. In this way, Moore helps to explain why Kant himself often seems to take what Moore calls 'the ironic step back' to the recognition of believing something false; and yet, Kant always ends up giving the impression that he has not done so.

Let us, briefly, restate how belief in immortality (similar to belief in God) is distinct from belief that there is a future life (or, that God exists)

Belief in God, on this way of construing it, is to be characterized by what it enables us to do, not by its content.[18]

We have found it extremely useful as philosophers to think, 'belief in God', but also belief in immortality, are like belief in rationality. Similar to a rational conviction, belief in . . . enables us to do virtuous acts, but it is not determined by empirical content. In other words, 'belief in God and confidence in morality grow out of the same metaphysical soil.'[19]

Corruption and Freedom: 'Is heaven our kind of place?'

Kant thought that if we are praised as good and condemned as evil, it is presupposed that we are free and rational. If one is condemned as evil, for having done something, one must have made a rational choice to perform that action, and that rational choice must have been made in accordance with an evil maxim. One is blamed because the maxim from which one acted was evil. If one's action is simply driven by external influences, one should not be blamed.[20] One may, for instance, just *happen* to undergo some urge to perform an evil action, but one should only be blamed for *rationally choosing* to succumb to the urge.

Kant thinks that we are all evil to some extent; that is, not all our rational actions are performed out of respect for the moral law. In fact, he thinks that we are all subject to what he calls 'radical evil'. The origin of our evil goes to the roots of our choice. We have somehow (timelessly?) chosen to have the capacity to be influenced by those natural inclinations resisting the moral law. This is described, contentiously, as a 'noumenal choice' which, even if think-able, would have to been unknowable, since not within the time-space bounds of the empirical world.[21]

Given our moral corruption, the question arises as to how we can be saved. This could be described as how we could be 'accepted into heaven'. But Kant's implicit conception of heaven was far from what might be called an everyday one. The latter conception of heaven might be roughly as follows:

'Heaven' is a place where it is obvious that any person would choose to go if one could only get there – a place where there is no punishment. The crucial question is how, given that one deserves punishment rather than heaven, one can get there. Perhaps God might be persuaded to waive the punishment and let one in, even though one remains sinful.[22]

It is clear that Kant does not hold the above view of heaven. In order to avoid confusion, Kant writes very little of 'heaven'. Instead he writes of how we can become 'pleasing to God'. In fact, salvation is, for Kant, 'becoming a human being well-pleasing to God'.[23] One cannot go to heaven and not deserve it.

It is conceivable that sinful persons would decide that becoming well-pleasing to God is not the goal of life. They might decide that heaven is just not their kind of place; they might be persuaded to change their minds. But their freedom and autonomy would be undermined if they were suddenly saved. This sudden happening would undermine the sinner's freedom, rationality and what is holy in the will. Kant cannot claim literally that God could make us worthy, for such a change from bad to good would be a result of (His) external influences. If so, then the sinner would not be worthy of anything.

So, without believing in an unmerited gift of salvation, as an unconditional form of grace, what precisely is Kant doing with references to Christ in the *Religion*? Kant's theory looks as though it might be heretical in what he is saying about humans striving to become well-pleasing to God, in not relying (solely) on God's grace and salvation in Christ. Nevertheless, it is not obvious that a charge of heresy cannot be answered. A supporter of what appears to be Kant's theory might hold that the narrative of Christ's life and death are necessary *to make sense* of salvation. The sinner also has to do something substantial, namely, to accept the forgiveness represented by Christ who, as prototype, enables us to recognize that we have fallen short of 'the archetype of the good moral disposition', and this makes it *possible* to repent of our wrong-doing, and to hope to perform a radical, yet mysteriously conceived 'change of heart'.[24] To remains central to Kant's moral religion, as well as to the role of salvation in Kant's thinking and writing.

Now, Henry Allison also addresses the struggle both to understand and to overcome radical evil, including in its social dimensions.[29] But, for Allison, the problem of self-deception is linked to questions about how human frailty leads to a self-incurred ignorance, or 'immaturity', which can spiral into total, that is, personal, social and metaphysical corruption. Allison agrees that 'Kant endeavours to show how the bare propensity to evil can account for extreme evil as a cultural phenomenon'. Also, similar to Wood, Allison addresses the initial connection between innocent self-love and the social context which are harmless until self-conceit is ignited by social corruption and eventually manifests the tie between self-deception and 'the most horrible crimes'.[30] Allison looks at how we can recognize the role of self-deception functioning in the escalation of evil as radical, but at origin, inscrutable.

In the end, though, if we are following Kant, and the argument developed in *Kant and Theology*, salvation cannot be achieved by an imitation of Christ who is represented without excessive self-love or self-deception. In contrast, our efforts can seem vain attempts: we never know when we have achieved the highest good, or salvation, nor can salvation be known as a gracious gift from a transcendent God. So, we are back to facing the harsh reality of the Kantian two-aspect subject. The autonomous subject must think, act and strive for a goal that is always just out of reach. Nevertheless, we have a shared rationality which will unite us in this struggle.

We might be cynical or simply unclear about this belief in a universally shared rationality, especially unclear about 'Christ's' role. Daniel Whistler makes some fine distinctions for us here:

[O]nly when mediated through his pedagogical relation to the world can Christ make his moral disposition evident to other subjects, and only then can he *both* exist

avoid heresy, salvation need not be considered simply a matter of God. To quote from Part One of Kant's *Religion within the Boundaries of Mere Reason*:

For here too the principle holds, 'It is not essential, and hence not necessary, that every human being know what God does, or has done, for his salvation'; but it is essential to know *what a human being has to do himself* in order to become worthy of this assistance.[25]

As we pointed out earlier, Kant thought that we are all, to some extent, evil; that is, some of the maxims from which we act are evil ones. This evil is radical, since it indicates that our very characters – that is, dispositions – are corrupt. We should repent and set about replacing the evil maxims of our action with good ones, hoping to become worthy of virtue rewarded with happiness, that is, the highest good. For Kant, then, salvation is a process of struggle and striving. This process of replacing our evil maxims with good ones will take, according to Part One of *Religion within Boundaries of Mere Reason*, an infinite amount of life. We obviously do not reach the end of this process in our temporal lives on, so to speak, 'earth'. So, we should suppose that we will be able to continue this striving in a future life; that is, immortality, as already defended. An infinite, yet apparently temporal process of improvement has as its ultimate (non-temporal) goal of being, metaphorically, well-pleasing to God. Once embarked on this process, we are free at any point to turn aside, or repent, and say that course is not for us.

But now a worry sets in. Suppose that we have attained salvation; that is, suppose that all of our maxims of action are good ones. How can we ever be certain that those are our maxims of action?[26] We cannot observe what these maxims of action are. We can only make a judgement as to which maxims we have in the light of our actions.

If I accept a bribe, then it might be reasonable to conclude that I have acted from an evil maxim. But if I do not accept the bribe, I cannot be sure that I am not acting from an evil maxim. I might just not have been offered enough money. One can never be sure that one has purified one's maxims of action. But also I may have done nothing wrong for a hundred years. And then, any satisfaction that I gain from that lack of wrong-doing can be dashed when I willingly commit a crime in the hundred and first year.

According to this interpretation of Kant on corruption and freedom, 'heaven' would have to be a rather insecure – virtually, mythical – place. After life's trials, a sinner is free to repent of wrong-doing at any point and adopt the moral process of becoming good; but the same sinner is equally free subsequently to reject that process. And even if one could have achieved salvation, Kant held that a human (sinner) can never be certain that this is so. Even in eternal life, one is deprived of any certainty. Kant hoped that, even though *we* will wonder whether we have achieved salvation, God, who is conceived imaginatively or, mythically as outside time, might Himself as non-human observe our maxims of action and judge us as saved.

Christ and Human Salvation

Ultimately, whatever 'salvation' brings to our minds in reading Kant (perhaps, a new heavenly life), it must come from our own human effort and striving to become as rational and so, as moral as possible. And yet, we know both that evil is radical and its origin is inscrutable. So, how do we make sense of the conundrums facing us in Kant's *Religion* – between the weak role of Christ as the God-man in salvation and our human failure ever to arrive with certainty on the other side of either personal or social corruption? Recent interpretations of Kant's conception of radical evil are insightful for the way in which they address the social dimensions of corruption, while also acknowledging the significant problems with claiming that the frailty of a human will leads to serious social as much as personal corruption.

Allen W. Wood argues that radical evil is 'a propensity of human reason' and develops 'under social conditions'. This is significant since Wood is not assuming that the Kantian subject is an isolated individual as implied by contemporary critiques of Kantian autonomy; the rational autonomous agent is not someone who struggles on her own for a mythical heaven; but autonomous subjects are bound together by the rationality which gives Kant's moral religion its distinctive holiness. In Wood's words,

> The propensity to self-conceit corrupts all human inclinations and affections, making them expressions of unsociable sociability. But self-conceit is evil only because it is opposed to the moral law of reason, which is the only power in human life capable of radically combating radical evil.
>
> . . . As the unconditioned capacity to make choices, reason is also the faculty through which we become aware of all values, and . . . this makes rational beings aware of the dignity of rational nature as an end in itself.
>
> . . . Kant holds that human beings can accomplish the tasks set by reason only by communicating with others. Our capacity to think at all, and especially to think accurately, depends on our thinking 'in community wi others to whom we communicate our thoughts, and who communicate their thoughts to us'.[27] Kant therefore concludes that 'reason depends for its very existence on the freedom to communicate'.[28]

Thus Kant, at least according to Wood, gives a signifi profound role to reason in 'communicating with oth practical reasoning in community also requires free this requirement for the freedom to communicate v

objectively *and* remain an exemplar to be followed. Exemplarity is only possible on the basis of teaching.[31]

Whistler's reading finds support in Kant's provision for our connection to Christ, when reason communicates to reason, via New Testament pedagogical discourse in the *Religion*:

> [W]hen expressed in thought as the ideal of humankind, such a disposition [as the ideal of goodness in Christ] . . . is perfectly valid for all human beings, at all times, and in all worlds, before the highest righteousness, whenever a human being makes his own like unto it, as he ought . . . [A]n appropriation of it for the sake of our own [disposition] must be possible, provided that ours is associated with the disposition of the prototype [Christ], even though rendering this appropriation comprehensible to us is still fraught with great difficulties.[32]

We can become good by 'appropriation' of Christ's goodness when expressed intellectually, that is, in his teachings. In turn, we imitate what is taught rather than what Christ is. This supports the process of becoming good, striving for the highest good. Yet, as Whistler adds,

> while another's good *action* can never be exemplary for us, through another's *thought of the good* we can learn to be good ourselves – since that proceeds directly from their reason to our reason, without being corrupted by realisation in the sensible realm.[33]

So, in *Kant and Theology*, we are keen to follow Whistler's rather neo-Platonic picture of Kant in separating out 'the sensible realm' as 'corrupted', while still requiring negotiation of the two aspects of Kant's subject between intelligible freedom and sensible corruption. Our distinctive aim is to conclude that for Kant salvation, even so to speak, in Christ moves from (His) reason to our reason as schematized, that is, placed into human time, in the archetype of the good moral disposition. This grounds a rational hope for, symbolically speaking, heaven as our kind place.

Critical Reception of Kantian Autonomy: Or, A Lesson for Theologians

Obstacles to Kant: Autonomy as Sinful and Masculine Pride

A close look at the reception of Kant's moral and religious philosophy in the present and previous century, especially critical reception of his conception of autonomy, by feminists and by 'post-secular' theologians, but also by traditional theists can provide us with the interpretative tools to challenge the account of autonomous reasoning which has, arguably, culminated in an damaging caricature of Kant.[1] There are lessons to be learnt here by theologians, as well as by other thinkers who quickly dismiss 'Kantian' autonomy. Seyla Benhabib clearly indicates the nature of this caricature which has dominated a rejection of Kant by theologians and non-theologians from a great variety of backgrounds. In Benhabib's words,

> Kant's error was to assume that I, as a pure rational agent reasoning for myself, could reach a conclusion that would be acceptable for all at all times and places. In Kantian moral theory, moral agents are like geometricians in different rooms who, reasoning alone for themselves, all arrive at the same solution to a problem.[2]

But is this strictly speaking 'Kant's error'? Is geometry the model for Kant's practical reasoning and the rational agent in the second *Critique*, or for moral religion in his *Religion*? Alternatively, is this an error made not by Kant, but by contemporary interpretations of moral agents in Kant? A damaging construal of his eighteenth-century conception of autonomy in terms of a formalist reasoning, or, we might say the theoretical reasoning of 'science', as in geometry (as cited above), preoccupy utilitarian and deontologist debates in twentieth-century normative ethics. Arguably, this assumed an overly abstract and de-contextualized reading of the rational agent in Kant; and this failed to maintain what we have advocated as the 'best' philosophical interpretation; that is, the two-aspects of Kant's subject of moral action.

In the late twentieth century, feminist philosophers and moral theologians developed decisive criticisms of Kant on the above construal of Kant's autonomous agent, despite what Kant actually wrote about reason and desire.[3] Feminist suspicion alone concludes that, from the beginning of Kant's critiques, there is something deeply problematic for women – and for some men at least – in 'his' conception of pure reason. Reason's supposed independence from, but also its capacity to order, the realm of nature seemed to exclude the bodily experiences of women and some men from the appropriation of reasoning in morality – let alone, reasoning in moral religion.[4] We must take seriously such criticisms, but also, the potential in critically restoring Kant's philosophy by recognizing necessary distinctions between the reasoning of geometry and practical reason.

In turning to Kant's *Critique of Practical Reason*, in Chapter 2 (above) it was helpful to focus upon a particular, salient example, in order to open up various questions concerning human reason, inclination, duty and autonomy.[5] This opening gave a space for reflection on the limited character of self-knowledge. For one thing, this necessitates the indirect interpretation of the social context and features of, to use again the phrase which derives from Spinoza, 'the effort and desire to be', of our rational striving.[6] For another thing, it raised the question of the nature of practical reasoning in Kant's example of a two-aspect moral subject.

Theologians against Autonomy: Learning a Lesson from Feminist Reformers

As seen in Chapter 4, ongoing reflection on such contemporary theological and philosophical concepts as autonomy needs to be both consistent generally with Kant and, in particular, with his thoughts on corruption. But at this stage our concern is consistency with contestations over his examples of autonomous reasoning on the grounds of gender, class, ethnicity and culture. With these obligations in mind we aim to contest the postmodern and post-secular claims of theologians in particular that the suppression of valuable texts by women and persons of a non-dominant race, class, ethnicity or sexual orientation cannot be properly reversed without rejecting the reason, or rationality, which constitutes what Kant calls holy in moral religion.

Admittedly, there remain unanswered questions, serious doubts, or objections to Kant's specifically male subject of inclination and duty who seeks autonomy. Debates in both philosophical and theological hermeneutics should be a means for the growth of less partial reasoning on practical and religious matters. Recall our reading of the example from the second *Critique* in Chapter 2 aims to establish the ongoing value of Kant's conception of human freedom and associated concepts. However, the question for many remains: without excluding women, non-Western men, with their distinctive theological and non-theological perspectives, can we affirm, the continuing prominence given to autonomy in 'Kantian' reasoning? Consistent with our account of Kant's moral religion, we can acknowledge the value of Kant in new readings of his morality which recognize the limits of our scientific knowledge and the nature of both theoretical and practical reasoning.[7] These potentials have been missed frequently both by what is excluded from a reading of his texts and by the way in which what has been included is read.[8]

So, a current demand on theologians is to interpret Kant's texts. Too often his examples have been read as if without any

material or social positioning in history, and without any understanding of 'reason' in Kant. In addition, to ignore the critical
role given to autonomy as a property of distinct rational agents
who, nevertheless, are sensible, temporal and so on, but equally
bound to each other by what they share – rationality – is to
ignore the role which Kant does give to the particularities
of embodiment, as well as to feelings such as sympathy or
empathy.[9] The danger is to concentrate strictly on the so-
called geometrical questions, say, in the universalizability of
maxims of good moral action in examples, such as the lying
promise in *The Groundwork of the Metaphysics of Morals*. To their
detriment, formalist readings of such examples in normative
ethics have tended to ignore both the particularities of our
sensible world and the interconnections of the meaning of
Kant's philosophical texts.

Critics of Kant in philosophy and theology continue to
assume that any concern with feelings and embodiment is
missing from Kant's normative ethics. They often fail to look
closely at his texts for what he says about reason and male–female
desire.[10] Appropriating the tools of theological hermeneutics,
readings of Kant can scrutinize the positive role given to the
autonomy of persons who remain in bodies and in need of a
certain moral – mutual – concern for each other's well-being.
A gesture towards a hermeneutical approach to Kant can be
found in various works of Continental philosophers and some
English-speaking women philosophers. For two examples,
consider a French philosopher like Paul Ricoeur, but also British
moral philosophers following Onora O'Neill: each has in her
or his own way helped the recognition and extension which
Kant himself gives to moral feeling, embodiment and imagination.[11] Political philosophers also recognize that in his *Critique
of the Power of Judgment* Kant achieves extensions of thought for
more concrete moral and political concerns.[12]

Basically, well-trained interpreters of Kant can discover the
possibility in his thinking in epistemology, ethics, metaphysics
and theology as valuable for contemporary interdisciplinary

debates. Relevant concepts in Kant for this include reason, desire, autonomy, logic, embodiment, judging and feeling, as well as the categories of judgements: universal, particular and singular. We think (with) these concepts and categories, in order to discover new gender-sensitive possibilities for Kant and moral religion. Scrutiny of the distortions, as well as the critical restorations, of Kant's moral religion can teach theologians today about what Kant finds 'holy' in humanity, and how to strive to be virtuous and so worthy of happiness. Consider the sense in which Kant's ideal of happiness is 'the reward' of virtue. It is perfectly represented in the archetype of the good moral disposition, that is, God in Christ.

> [I]t is our universal human duty to *elevate* ourselves to this ideal of moral perfection, i.e. to the prototype of moral disposition in its entire purity, and for this the very idea, which is presented to us by reason for emulation, can give us force.[13] In emulating the pure moral disposition, reason imitates Christ; such imitation is to 'steadfastly cling to the prototype of humanity and follow this prototype's example in loyal emulation'.[14]

To better understand both autonomous practical reasoning, and the role of Christ in Kant's moral religion we have been encouraging our readers to go back to his eighteenth-century texts before going forward in their theology and interdisciplinary thinking. A serious reclamation of Kantian autonomy returns to the *Groundwork*, the first, second and third *Critiques* and 'An Answer to the Question: "What is Enlightenment?"' The distinctive Kantian structure in his use of the three distinct categories of unity, plurality and totality include Kant's forms of judgement, his categories of pure understanding, his formulations of the categorical imperative and his maxims of common human understanding. Each of these is unified in triads (of unity, plurality and totality); yet they remain essentially distinct.

What is pivotal in Kant's three formulations of the categorical imperative appears in the long passage from the *Groundwork* (below). Notice, in particular, the role of bringing 'an idea [that is, the idea of moral law or autonomy] of reason closer to intuition and thereby to feeling'[15]:

> *Autonomy* is . . . the ground of the dignity of human nature and of every rational nature . . . The . . . three ways of representing the principle of morality are at bottom only so many formulae of the very same law, and any one of them of itself unites the other two in it. There is nevertheless a difference among them, which is indeed subjectively rather than objectively practical, intended namely to bring an idea of reason closer to intuition (by a certain analogy) and thereby to feeling. All maxims have, namely:
>
> 1) a *form*, which consists in universality; and in this respect the formula of the moral imperative is expressed thus: the maxims must be chosen as if they were to hold as universal laws of nature;
> 2) a *matter*, namely an end, and in this respect the formula says that a rational being, as an end by its nature and hence as an end in itself, must in every maxim serve as the limiting condition of all merely relative and arbitrary ends;
> 3) *a complete determination* of all maxims by means of that formula, namely that all maxims from one's own lawgiving are to harmonize with a possible kingdom of ends as with a kingdom of nature. A progression takes place here, as through the categories of the *unity* of form of the will (its universality), the *plurality* of the matter (of objects, that is of ends), and the *allness* or totality of the system of these [ends]. But one does better always to proceed in moral appraisal by the strict method and put at its basis the universal formula of the categorical

imperative: act in accordance with a maxim that can at
the same time make itself a universal law.[16]

The account (above) of the three formulations of the categorical imperatives is an outline for 'the kingdom of ends';
treating others as much as oneself as ends, and not mere means,
generates this kingdom – in which 'ends' could also be represented by the ideal of God, that is, the anticipated ideal of virtue
worthy of happiness. But several issues are raised concerning
the relationship of the different formulae for the same universal
law of humanity. There are three (or four depending on how
they are read) formulations of the categorical imperative. Yet the
crucial issue for *Kant and Theology* is, whether we should follow
Kant's claim (in the last sentence above) to give preference to
the 'strict method', or formula, for testing the universalizability
of the maxim of an action. Instead, to preserve the richness
of Kant's larger picture of transcendental idealism, the nature of
theoretical and practical reasoning, then Kant's thinking is not
reducible to what has become known as 'Kantian formalism', or
'rigorism'.[17] Restricting Kant to a universal formula for moral
maxims has resulted in the exclusiveness of a formalism in
which moral actions are only assessed according to the (internal) consistency of their maxims. More strongly stated, the
exclusiveness of the test for the universalizability of the maxims
of actions has at times plagued the reception of Kant's moral
philosophy, especially in the twentieth century. In contrast, a
more nuanced reading of Kant's overall picture of autonomy
retrieves a Kantian architectonic, in which the *form* (unity),
matter (plurality) and *totality* (universality) of ends are constantly
in view.[18]

It is crucial for theologians who seek to follow Kant that the
principle of autonomy becomes a moral imperative for religion, with ethical, political and aesthetic dimensions. We should,
'dare to learn, taste and savour for [ourselves]'!'[19] Essentially the
various versions of Kant's moral imperative culminate in, 'Think

for yourself' (*Sapere aude*). This supports the centrality of autonomy to Kant's political writings, as well as to critical claims concerning reason.[20] Kant himself intends to submit all claims to the free examination of reason. In his words:

> Reason must subject itself to critique in all its undertakings, and cannot restrict the freedom of critique through any prohibition without damaging itself and drawing upon itself a disadvantageous suspicion. Now there is nothing so important because of its utility, nothing so holy, that it may be exempted from this searching review and inspection, which knows no respect for persons. The very existence of reason depends upon this freedom, which has no dictatorial authority, but whose claim is never anything more than the agreement of free citizens, each of whom must be able to express his reservations, indeed even his *veto*, without holding back.[21]

In the above, the autonomous use of reason cannot be a matter of detachment or dis-embedded thinking. Kant's critiques of reason themselves place autonomy in the context of concrete life where critical scrutiny by other subjects cannot be avoided.[22] The very existence of reason depends upon autonomy, but autonomy is only realized in the employment of reason practically. It is important to bear in mind this practically embedded and embodied nature of Kantian reasoning, despite its contemporary critics.

Kant's Philosophical Contribution to Theological Hermeneutics

Kant's critical philosophy opened the door to philosophical hermeneutics. In rejecting the possibility of (absolute) knowledge of God, freedom and immortality, Kant paved the route to an indirect method of interpretation of morality, the self and temporal/non-temporal life. In so doing he renders partial the knowledge we can have of ourselves, including the partiality in our knowledge of autonomous action. On one level, this epistemological partiality renders us vulnerable to a 'radical' and 'inscrutable' evil which 'corrupts' the ground of our maxims by subverting the rationality of our good maxims. Basically, we might be wrong about what we know and what is right precisely because 'evil' is radical and we cannot know its real origin. On another level, we are also vulnerable as embodied to pain, suffering and death. Theologians after Kant who go down the road of applying their method of 'theological hermeneutics' to Kant's texts might discover that hermeneutics itself gained its autonomy after Kant in practical reasoning.[23] As discussed and illustrated in Chapter 2 (above), hermeneutics is the technical term for a practice which is no longer restricted in its scope to the biblical text, or to privileged practitioners. Theological hermeneutics intends to reject the alternative of relative or absolute knowledge, going with Kant to think beyond the bounds of empirical knowledge, by continuing to think both beyond the knowable and for oneself. Ironically, this unites us in what is holy in humanity.

Equally the danger of the contemporary trends in theology and morality is perhaps ironic; it is both relativism and absolutism. These are actually two sides of the same coin inasmuch as the choice of hermeneutics is a rejection of absolutism, it is equally a rejection of moral relativism. But this implies that assertions of absolutism merely relativize the position of the absolutists. This reflects the spirit of Kant who rejects all dogmatism. Imagine Kant today. Surely he would call our contemporary relativists 'the dogmatists' who inherit the reductive thinking. The current exigency is clearly to render the twenty-first century a period of restorative thinking, with more nuanced, hermeneutic sensibilities, notably towards Kant and theology.

To conclude with critics who have tried to disclaim Kantian autonomy in thought and action, let us return to the feminist hermeneutic critiques of the disembodied and dis-embedded self. Notable is the moral psychologist Carol Gilligan who gained great fame in the 1970s, not only in psychology but in theology, ethics, politics and gender studies for her critique of autonomy as the goal in Lawrence Kohlberg's theory of moral development; and so likewise, in John Rawls and the Kantian moral and political theories of the day.[24] In fact, Benhabib's reformist approach to Enlightenment morality, mentioned at the outset of this chapter, responds to Gilligan's critique of Kantian morality and conceives moral subject(s) in terms of both the generalized and the concrete other.[25] This advances beyond the antagonism between conceptions of the generalized and the concrete, the public and the domestic, autonomy and nurturance. Yet Benhabib's post-Kantian approach has, in turn, been criticized by the feminist political philosopher Iris Marion Young for failing to recognize the asymmetry in reciprocity between subjects.[26] This generates further debates after Kant. Yet the philosophical argument of Ricoeur's *petite éthique*, in *Oneself as Another*, offers a Kantian, mediating position between Benhabib and Young. Ricoeur has an affinity to Benhabib's post-Kantian account of the other, while recognizing, not unlike Young's asymmetry, an inevitable 'dissymmetry' between subjects as agent and patient.[27] Such a mediating position between conflicting feminist interpretations of the subject in Kant provides a significant alternative for twenty-first-century theologians to return and think as Kant suggests for themselves when it comes to too hasty dismissals of Kant.

The intention of this chapter has been to consider the reception of Kant, especially a misconstrual and so dismissal of his thinking by theologians and post-modern critical theorists. In response, we have urged a retrieval of autonomy, especially from its distortions and disclaimers by an age of moral relativism. This is the post-modern age which has celebrated concrete identities, but assumed that the universal (or general) standpoint of autonomy represents an un-free reason, for example, of geometric formulae. Over and against the post-modern, *Kant and Theology* demonstrates the great value in reclaiming Kantian autonomy for those who reject the disembodied and disembedded self of twentieth-century theology and formalist work in philosophy of religion. Kant offers insights into philosophical and theological debates concerning the critique, retrieval and insightful reconfiguration of a principled autonomy. Some ethicists have presented what have seemed to be decisive criticisms of autonomy in moral and political philosophy, while other Kantian friendly philosophers seek to retrieve autonomy's social and global possibilities for every discipline today.[28] Taken together overly dismissive receptions of Kant do not constitute enough reasons for abandoning autonomy full-stop. Instead Kant's moral religion in particular can still support autonomy's role as an ideal for a kingdom of ends (God).[29] The important contribution of feminists to debates on Kant's moral religion is to reveal the need to rethink normative conceptions of the self, especially a popular conception of the autonomous self which has, for some, represented exclusively male attributes. This normative conception has weakened Kantian ethics, distorting Kant's own account of autonomy. This has left theology cut off from the real possibilities in theoretical and practical debates about God, goodness, sin and salvation after Kant.

The constructive element in the autonomous use of reason in theology involves freely and actively building the constructions of practical reason, as opposed to submitting to norms which are alien to our humanity. O'Neill offers an impressive summary of Kant's maxim of autonomy in its constructive role of 'common human understanding'.[30] O'Neill's reflection builds upon the *Critique of the Power of Judgment* as follows:

> . . . Only those who think for themselves have any contribution to make to a debate or plan. Those who suppress their own voices do not reason; they are mere voiceless echoes, whose parroted words cannot be taken as expressions of judgment or as acts of communication. Those who elide their own status as thinkers among

other thinkers cannot adhere to the categorical imperative; they do not reason, and are doomed to disorientated consciousness . . .

Those who reject this discipline no longer seek to interact or communicate; they are not committed to the maintenance or the development of any sharable modes of disciplining thought or action, and so may find their supposed reasoning impenetrable to others.[31]

The above expresses well the necessary role of Kantian autonomy for uniting rational agents in what we have found to be schematized in 'Christ' and the 'kingdom of God'; these are symbolic analogies to the ideals of human morality and moral religion; and as such, pivotal for Kant's contribution to theology.

Kant tells each of us to think for ourselves, in order to communicate and to share norms of acting, thinking and reasoning with others. Theoretically and practically, autonomy and its own complement of vulnerability to other subjects and to the points of view of other subjects would seem to be the correct spirit for the critical use of reason in theology and in theological debates with other disciplines, as well as with and between non-theist religions.

Conclusion

In 'An Answer to the Question: "What is Enlightenment?"' Kant thinks of his age as a time when humans are starting to think for themselves, but Enlightenment had not yet been achieved. And one of the greatest dangers of his age for theologians – which some of us today might contend is true today, too – is, according to Kant, 'self-incurred immaturity'. In his words,

If it is now asked whether we at present live in an enlightened age, the answer is: No, but we do live in an age of enlightenment. As things are at present, we still have a long way to go before men [sic] as a whole can be in a position (or can even be put into a position) of using their own understanding confidently and well in religious matters, without outside guidance. But ... the way is now being cleared for them to work freely in this direction, and that the obstacles to universal enlightenment, to man's self-incurred immaturity, are gradually becoming fewer.[32]

Today we continue to try to think for ourselves and there is no reason to think – despite the post-modern cries to the contrary – that we have, or should have, stopped the moral development of our thinking and acting. Insofar as the Enlightenment of humanity matures and moves us forward, Kant continues to be as significant a figure for theology, morality, epistemology and aesthetics in the twenty-first century as he was in the eighteenth.

Notes

Epigraph

1. Cf. Immanuel Kant, *Critique of Pure Reason*. Translated by Norman Kemp Smith (London: Macmillan, 1933), p. 257 (A235–236/ B294–295).
2. Michèle Le Doeuff, *The Philosophical Imaginary*. Translated by Colin Gordon (London: The Athlone Press, 1989; London: Continuum, 2002), pp. 14–16.

Introduction

1. Manfred Kuehn, *Kant: A Biography* (Cambridge: Cambridge University Press, 2001), p. 26.
2. Admittedly, there is some irony in this 'pride' since, as we will demonstrate, Kant might hold a belief, or even 'confidence', in God; but he could never claim knowledge that 'God is with him'.
3. Kuehn, *Kant*, p. 31. Cf. Immanuel Kant, *Gesammelte Schriften*, vol. 13. *Ausgabeder Königlich preussischen Akademie der Wissenschaften* (Berlin: W. de Gruyter, 1900–), p. 461.
4. Philip Jakob Spener, *Pia desideria*. Translated, edited and with an Introduction by Theodore G. Tappert (Philadelphia, PA: Fortress Press, 1964).
5. For some helpful historical background to Kant's 'rational theology' in Pietism, Lutheran theology and Enlightenment rationalism, see Allen W. Wood, 'Rational Theology, Moral Faith and Religion', in Paul Guyer, ed. *The Cambridge*

Companion to Kant (Cambridge: Cambridge University Press, 1992), pp. 394–399.

6. Bernard M. G. Reardon makes this connection between Zinzendorf and Wesley in *Kant as Philosophical Theologian* (London: Macmillan Press, 1988), p. 188n3; also, on the Pietist movement, pp. 4–7. For Wesley's translations of hymns by Zinzendorf, see *Pietists: Selected Writings*. Edited with an Introduction by Peter C. Erb, and a Preface by F. Ernest Stoeffler (London: SPCK, 1983), pp. 301–303.

7. Kuehn, *Kant*, p. 51.

8. Ibid.

9. Allen W. Wood, *Kant*. Blackwell Great Minds (Oxford: Blackwell, 2005), pp. 4–8. Wood gives as an example of Kant's negative views, his definition of 'pietist' as someone who 'tastelessly makes the idea of religion dominant in all conversation and discourse' (p. 4). Cf. Immanuel Kant, *Gesammelte Schriften*, vol. 27. *Ausgabe der Königlich Preussischen Akademie der Wissenschaften* (Berlin: W. de Gruyter, 1902), p. 23. This, Wood says, is one of Kant's mildest remarks about Pietism.

10. Wood, 'Rational Theology, Moral Faith and Religion', p. 396.

11. Here Kant means Frederick the Great; cf. Immanuel Kant, 'An Answer to the Question: What is Enlightenment?' in *Kant: Political Writings*. Translated by H. B. Nisbet. Edited with an Introduction and Notes by Hans Reiss (Cambridge: Cambridge University Press, 1991), p. 58.

12. Kuehn, *Kant*, p. 97.

13. Ibid., p. 117.

14. Ibid., p. 154; cf. Karl Hagen, 'Kantiana', *Neue Preussische Provincial-Blätter* 6 (1848): 9.

15. Kuehn, *Kant*, p. 155.

16. Both Wöllner's letter and Kant's reply were published by Kant himself in the Preface to the *Conflict of the Faculties* (1798), in *Religion and Rational Theology* (Cambridge: Cambridge University Press, 1996), pp. 239–242.

Chapter 1

1. Immanuel Kant, *Critique of Pure Reason*. Translated by Norman Kemp Smith (London: Macmillan, 1933), p. 93 (A 51).
2. Ibid., p. 22 (Bxvi).
3. Frederick Copleston, *A History of Philosophy,* vol. 6, *The Enlightenment: Voltaire to Kant* (London: 1960; London and New York: Continuum, 2003).
4. For a clear introduction to this debate, including two different interpretations of the distinction between appearances and things in themselves, see Allen W. Wood, *Kant*. Blackwell Great Minds (Oxford: Blackwell, 2005), pp. 63–76.
5. The reader may find historic discussions of the debates between the two-world and two-aspect interpretations in H. E. Matthews [1969], 'Strawson on Transcendental Idealism' in Ralph C. S. Walker, eds. *Kant on Pure Reason.* Oxford Readings in Philosophy (Oxford: Oxford University Press, 1982), pp.132–149; and T. E. Wilkerson, *Kant's Critique of Pure Reason* (Oxford: Clarendon Press, 1976). One of the most famous two-world interpreters is P. F. Strawson, *Bounds of Sense: An Essay on Kant's Critique of Pure Reason* (London: Methuen & Co. Ltd., 1966). The current leading advocate of the two-aspect interpretation is Henry E. Allison, *Kant's Transcendental Idealism: An Interpretation and Defense* (New Haven: Yale University Press, 1983); *Kant's Theory of Freedom* (Cambridge: Cambridge University Press, 1990); *Idealism and Freedom: Essays on Kant's Theoretical and Practical Philosophy* (Cambridge: Cambridge University Press, 1996).
6. Later we will add the distinction between 'belief that' and 'belief in', in order to explain how we can have knowledge of theoretical matters, but only postulates of practical reason.
7. Kant, *Critique of Pure Reason*, p. 257 (A235–236/ B294–295). The metaphor of 'the island' and the imagery of a

'territory of pure understanding' are crucial for Kant's 'Transcendental Analytic', Book Two: 'Analytic of Principles', Chapter Three: 'The Ground of the Distinction of all Objects in General into Phenomena and Noumena', *Critique of Pure Reason*, pp. 257–275.

8. Ibid., Bxxviii.
9. Ibid., Bxxix italics added.
10. Ibid., A26/B42 italics added.
11. 'God' in this theoretical context, that is, as an idea in Kant's first *Critique*, could not be conceived as anything in time or space, since anything temporal and/or spatial is a human construct. Basically, we accept that God, according to Kant's theoretical reasoning, could not be an object, a cause or anything else in time. This also means that God is unknowable.
12. For a detailed account of freedom and its place both in Kant's theory of transcendental idealism and in the development of Kant's and post-Kantian philosophy, see Michelle Kosch, *Freedom and Reason in Kant, Schelling and Kierkegaard* (Oxford: Oxford University Press, 2006), pp. 15–44.
13. Again, this reason, that is, to act for the sake of duty alone, will be discussed in Chapter 2 with discussion of Immanuel Kant, *Groundwork of the Metaphysics of Morals*. Translated by Mary Gregor. Introduction by Christine M. Korsgaard (Cambridge: Cambridge University Press, 1998), pp. 3–4, 10–14 (4.390, 4.397–401); also see, *The Moral Law: Kant's Groundwork of the Metaphysic of Morals*. Translated and analysed by H. J. Paton (London: Hutchinson, 1951), pp. 18–19 and 63.
14. Kant, *Critique of Pure Reason*, Bxxviii (also, above a reference to the quotation from the text appears in endnote 8).

Chapter 2

1. Thanks are due to James Carter for discussions of Kant's moral religion, especially in relation to moral psychology,

and its significance for contemporary theology. For his own work on Kant, see James Carter, 'Moral Religion: Ethics, Hermeneutics and Life,' University of Oxford DPhil Thesis, forthcoming.

2. Immanuel Kant, *Critique of Practical Reason*. Translated by Mary Gregor (Cambridge: Cambridge University Press, 1997), p. 74 (5.87). For an alternative reading of Kant's theory of practical reasoning (that is, as only a, not the, central concern of Kant's philosophy), see the account of the central role of the imagination in 're-enchanting' our humanity, see Jane Kneller, *Kant and the Power of Imagination* (Cambridge: Cambridge University Press, 200), pp. 25–30.

3. Immanuel Kant, *Groundwork of the Metaphysics of Morals*. Translated and edited by Mary Gregor with an Introduction by Christine M. Korsgaard (Cambridge: Cambridge University Press, 1997), p. 58 (4.453). For more on reason and its relations to sensibility and understanding, see p. 57 (4.452).

4. Immanuel Kant, *Groundwork of the Metaphysics of Morals*. Translated by Mary Gregor with an Introduction by Christine M. Korsgaard (Cambridge: Cambridge University Press, 1997), pp. 52–53 (4.447).

5. Kant, *The Groundwork of the Metaphysics of Morals*, pp. 10–16 (4:397–404).

6. On Kant's categorical imperative, see *Groundwork of the Metaphysics of Morals*, pp. 30–31, 42–44 (4:420–436) and 58–59 (4.453–4.455).

7. For a reading of Allen Wood's early and later views of Kant as 'moral theism' and 'deism', respectively, see Chris L. Firestone and Nathan Jacobs, *In Defense of Kant's Religion* (Bloomington, IN: Indiana University Press, 2008), especially pp. 36–38, 77–78. For a reading of Kant as helping to bring about nineteenth-century atheism, rather than liberal Protestant theology, see George Michalson, *Kant and the Problem of God* (Oxford: Blackwell, 1999).

8. On Pietism, see *Pietists: Selected Writings*. Edited with an Introduction by Peter C. Erb, and a Preface by F. Ernest Stoeffler (London: SPCK, 1983); Bernard M. G. Reardon, *Kant as Philosophical Theologian* (London: Macmillan Press, 1988), pp. 4–7; and Manfred Kuehn, *Kant: A Biography* (Cambridge: Cambridge University Press, 2001). Also see the Introduction within this book.
9. Cf. Kant, *Critique of Practical Reason*, p. 74 (5.87) and pp. 109–110 (5.131).
10. Kant, *Groundwork of the Metaphysics of Morals*, p. 21 (4:408).
11. Ibid., pp. 57–58 (4.452–453).
12. Ibid.; and Kant, *Critique of Practical Reason*, pp. 38–43 (5.42–5.49).
13. Kant, *Critique of Practical Reason*, p. 133 (5.161–162).
14. See endnote 5 (above). Also, see Onora O'Neill, *Constructions of Reason: Explorations of Kant's Practical Philosophy* (Cambridge: Cambridge University Press, 1989), pp. 126–144.
15. Immanuel Kant, *Religion within the Boundaries of Mere Reason*. Translated and edited by George di Giovanni and Allen Wood with an Introduction by Robert Merrihew Adams (Cambridge: Cambridge University Press, 1998), pp. 80 (6.61) and 91n* (6.75).
16. Allen W. Wood has a keen sense of this irony – that twentieth-century theologians and religious believers have a deep suspicion of Kant as 'immoral' because of his conception of autonomy, or 'individualism' – both of which are misconceptions; but Kant would be equally critical of the 'immorality' and 'degradation' of his accusers, especially those who find the Enlightenment 'bad', see Allen W. Wood, *Kant's Ethical Thought* (Cambridge: Cambridge University Press, 1999), pp. 319–320.
17. Ibid., p. 319.
18. Kant, *Religion with the Boundaries of Mere Reason*, p. 85 (6.67–68) and p. 105 (6.93); cf. Kant, *Critique of Practical Reason*, pp. 41–47 (4.433–4.440).

19. Roughly, the analytic scrutinizes the role of truth in its principles (for example, of empirical causality) by unpacking or deducing the central concepts of pure practical reason; in contrast, the dialectic exposes the role of illusion by demonstrating how it is that human thinking continues to seek, while never being able to achieve, the totality of all conditions (that is, the unconditioned); see Kant, *Critique of Practical Reason*.

20. Kant, *Critique of Pure Reason*, p. 475n[a] (A552/B580).

21. Paul Ricoeur, *Freud and Philosophy: An Essay on Interpretation*. Translated by Denis Savage (New Haven and London: Yale University Press, 1970), pp. 45–46; and Pamela Sue Anderson, 'On Loss of Confidence: Dissymmetry, Doubt, Deprivation in the Power to Act and (the Power) to Suffer', in Daniel Whistler, James Carter and Joseph Carlisle, eds. *Moral Powers, Fragile Beliefs: Essays in Moral and Religious Philosophy* (London and New York: Continuum, 2010).

22. On the 'sole fact' of (pure) reason, see Kant, *Critique of Practical Reason*, pp. 28–9 and 37 (5: 31 and 5:42).

23. Kant, *Critique of Practical Reason*, pp. 27–28 (5:31).

24. Ibid., p. 42 (5:47).

25. For feminist readings of this objectification, see Barbara Herman, 'Could It Be Worth Thinking About Kant on Sex and Marriage', and Sally Haslanger, 'On Being Objective and Being Objectified', in Louise M. Antony and Charlotte Witt, eds. *A Mind of One's Own: Feminist Essays on Reason and Objectivity* (Oxford: Westview Press, 1993), pp. 49–68 and 85–126, respectively. Rae Langton. 'Feminism in Epistemology: Exclusion and Objectification', in *The Cambridge Companion to Feminism in Philosophy*, pp. 127–145.

26. Martha C. Nussbaum, 'Objectification', in *Sex and Social Justice* (Oxford: Oxford University Press, 1999), pp. 213–239. For more on objectification in relation to 'lust', see endnote 29 (below).

27. Immanuel Kant, *Critique of the Power of Judgment*. Translated by Paul Guyer and Eric Matthews (Cambridge: Cambridge University Press, 2000), p. 175 (5.294–5.295).
28. Ibid., p. 174 (5.294). Also, see Paul Ricoeur, 'Appropriation', *Hermeneutics and the Human Sciences*. Translated by John B. Thompson (Cambridge: Cambridge University Press, 1981), pp. 182–193. Further discussion of Kant's maxims of autonomous thought from the third *Critique*, see the Conclusion, pp. 85–86.
29. For further discussion of Kant's account of sex, especially of the object of desire, see Herman, 'Could It Be Worth Thinking About Kant on Sex and Marriage', pp. 49–67. For a different reading of Kant which draws a significant distinction between pathological and practical love, see Susan Mendus, 'The Practical and Pathological', in Susan Mendus, *Feminism and Emotion: Readings in Moral and Political Philosophy* (London: Macmillan Press Ltd, 2000), pp. 43–54. Also, see Simon Blackburn, *Lust* (Oxford: Oxford University Press, 2006), pp. 93–97 and 139n60, n62.
30. These *Lectures on Ethics* were delivered in the 1760s, possibly written up in 1765–1766; compiled and published in German in 1924.
31. Immanuel Kant, *Lectures on Ethics*, trans. Louis Infield (New York: Harper Torchbooks, 1963), pp. 163–164.
32. O'Neill, 'The Power of Examples', in *Constructions of Reason*, pp. 165–186; and Onora O'Neill, *Towards Justice and Virtue: A Constructive Account of Practical Reasoning* (Cambridge: Cambridge University Press, 1996), pp. 85–89.
33. Onora O'Neill, *The Bounds of Justice* (Cambridge: Cambridge University Press, 2000), pp. 42–48.
34. There are, however, number of Anglo-American women moral philosophers who have begun a significant rereading and defence of Kant's ethics against critics who claim that his focus on the universal law forces Kantians to ignore particulars of context and differences in bodily nature. This impressive work on Kant represents the changing tide in

Kantian moral philosophy: in addition to Onora O'Neill, there are Barbara Herman, Christine M. Korsgaard and Nancy Sherman who have each played parts in redressing the balance of overly formalist readings of Kant's moral philosophy. See Barbara Herman, *The Practice of Moral Judgement* (Cambridge, MA: Harvard University Press, 1993); Christine M. Korsgaard, *The Sources of Normativity* (Cambridge: Cambridge University Press, 1996); and Nancy Sherman, *Making a Necessity of Virtue* (Cambridge: Cambridge University Press, 1997).

35. Kant, *Critique of Practical Reason*, pp. 26–29 (5.29–31); also see endnote 21 above.
36. David Jasper, *A Short Introduction to Hermeneutics* (Westminster John Knox Press, 2004), p. 1.
37. Ibid., pp. 1 and 3.
38. Ricoeur, *Freud and Philosophy,* pp. 20–36 and 42–56.
39. Genevieve Lloyd, 'Feminism in the History of Philosophy: Appropriating the Past', in Miranda Fricker and Jennifer Hornsby, eds. *The Cambridge Companion to Feminism in Philosophy* (Cambridge: Cambridge University Press, 2000), p. 253.

Chapter 3

1. Immanuel Kant, *Critique of Pure Reason.* Translated by Norman Kemp Smith (London: Macmillan, 1929), A568–577/B568–605.
2. Ibid., A571–2/B599–600.
3. Allen W. Wood helpfully situates Kant's conception of a supremely perfect being in a 'scholastic-rationalist tradition', see Wood, 'Rational Theology, Moral Faith and Religion', in Paul Guyer, ed. *The Cambridge Companion to Kant* (Cambridge: Cambridge University Press, 1992), pp. 398–405.
4. Kant, *Critique of Pure Reason,* A575/B603.

5. Ibid., A582/B610.
6. Ibid., A598/B626.
7. Ibid., A584/B612.
8. Ibid., A625/B653.
9. Ibid., A629/B657.
10. C. D. Broad, *Kant: An Introduction* (Cambridge: Cambridge University Press, 1978), p. 298.
11. Broad, *Kant*, p. 299.
12. Ibid.
13. Ibid.
14. Andrews Reath makes a helpful observation about the translations of *Vernunftglaube* as 'rational faith', or 'rational belief', even 'faith of practical reason', see his 'Introduction', in Immanuel Kant, *Critique of Practical Reason*. Translated by Mary Gregor (Cambridge: Cambridge University Press, 1997), p. *xiv* n6. For a concise discussion of *Glaube*, see Allen W. Wood, 'Rational Theology, Moral Faith, and Religion', in Paul Guyer, ed. *The Cambridge Companion to Kant* (Cambridge: Cambridge University Press, 1992), pp. 404–405.
15. For Kant's presentation of this argument, see Kant, *Critique of Practical Reason*, translated by Mary Gregor, pp. 90–93 (107–111); also see pp. 118–121 (5:143–146); cf. *Critique of Practical Reason*. Translated by Lewis White Beck (Indianapolis: The Bobbs-Merrill Co., 1956), pp. 111–114 (107–111); also see pp. 148–151 (143–146).
16. For another summary of the argument for the postulates, especially of 'the highest good' or God, see Reath, 'Introduction', in Kant, *Critique of Practical Judgement*. Translated by Mary Gregor, pp. xxviii–xxix.
17. In Chapter 4 (below), we return to discuss the significant distinction between 'belief in' and 'belief that', for Kant's practical reasoning and his moral religion.
18. Wood, 'Rational Theology, Moral Faith, and Religion', p. 404.

19. P. F. Strawson, *Bounds of Sense: An Essay on Kant's Critique of Pure Reason* (London: Methuen & Co. Ltd., 1966), pp. 16–18 and 35.

20. Kant, *Critique of Pure Reason*, A 426–432/B454–460.

21. For a range of other accounts of Kant's 'proofs' for the existence of God, see Peter Byrne, *Kant on God* (Aldershot, Hants: Ashgate Publishing Limited, 2007), pp. 19–56; Frederick Copleston, *A History of Philosophy. The Enlightenment: Voltaire to Kant* (London: 1960), pp. 294–307; Gordon E. Michalson, Jr. *Kant and the Problem of God* (Oxford: Blackwell, 1999), pp. 28–56. Wood, 'Rational Theology, Moral Faith and Religion', pp. 397–403.

22. A. W. Moore, *Noble in Reason, Infinite in Faculty: Themes and Variations in Kant's Moral and Religious Philosophy* (London: Routledge, 2003), pp. 155–158 and 188–189.

23. Moore, *Noble in Reason, Infinite in Faculty*, p. 188.

24. Gordon E. Michalson, Jr. *Fallen Freedom: Kant on Radical Evil and Moral Regeneration* (Cambridge: Cambridge University Press, 1990), p. 25.

Chapter 4

1. Immanuel Kant, *Religion within the Boundaries of Mere Reason and Other Writings*. Translated and edited by Allen Wood and George di Giovanni with an Introduction by Robert Merrihew Adams (Cambridge: Cambridge University Press, 1998), p. 186.

2. Ibid., p. 114 (6.105). Compare this statement in Kant's *Religion* to the paragraphs in Immanuel Kant, *Critique of Practical Reason*. Translated by Mary Gregor (Cambridge: Cambridge University Press, 1997), pp. 109–112 (5.131–5). For an argument about how to read apparently contradictory assumptions on this topic of 'divine commands', see Allen W. Wood, 'Rational Theology, Moral Faith and Religion', in Paul Guyer, ed. *The Cambridge Companion to*

Kant (Cambridge: Cambridge University Press, 1992), pp. 406–408.

3. Kant, *Religion*, p. 114.
4. Kant, *Religion*, p. 115. Also, for Kant's criticisms of practices of praying and of wiping sins away [by means of 'grace'] without moral effort, see pp. 188 and 189, respectively.
5. For a demonstration of the failure of purely speculative reason to construct a theology, see Kant, *Critique of Pure Reason*, A638/B666. For more on conviction and moral certainty, see Ibid., A828/B856; also, A820/B857.
6. These inverted commas are meant to raise a doubt as to whether or not this *is* Kant's.
7. Chris L. Firestone and Nathan Jacobs, *In Defense of Kant's Religion* (Bloomington, IN: Indiana University Press, 2008). Also see George di Giovanni, 'Reply to Firestone and Jacobs' *In Defence of Religion'*, *Journal of Religion*, Special Issue (2010), forthcoming.
8. Firestone and Jacobs, *In Defense of Kant's Religion*, pp. 112–115, 155, 168–170, 233–234.
9. Allen W. Wood, *Kant's Ethical Thought* (Cambridge: Cambridge University Press, 1999), p. 317 italics added.
10. Kant, *Religion within the Boundaries of Mere Reason*, pp. 45–73. Also see Wood, *Kant's Ethical Thought*, pp. 283–290.
11. Kant, *Religion within the Boundaries of Mere Reason*, pp. 190–191 (6: 201–202).
12. A. W. Moore, *Noble in Reason, Infinite in Faculty: Themes and Variations in Kant's Moral and Religious Philosophy* (London: Routledge, 2003), pp. 155–158.
13. Ibid., p. 156.
14. Recall our discussion of 'belief in,' see Chapter 3 (pp. 55, 58) and endnote 17 of that chapter.
15. Kant, *Religion within the Boundaries of Mere Reason*, pp. 159–160 (6:162).
16. Moore, *Noble in Reason*, p. 157.
17. Moore, *Noble in Reason*, pp. 166–167 italics added; cf. also see 192–193.

18. Moore, *Noble in Reason*, p. 189.
19. Gordon E. Michalson, *Fallen Freedom: Kant on Radical Evil and Moral Regeneration* (Cambridge: Cambridge University Press, 1990), p. 25.
20. For further discussion of the question, can a Kantian subject act freely and at the same time, do an evil act? See Michelle Kosch, *Freedom and Reason in Kant, Schelling and Kierkegaard* (Oxford: Oxford University Press, 2006), pp. 44–65. Kosch discusses critical reception of Kant's conception of moral evil by his own contemporaries and immediate predecessors.
21. For background on the problem of making the 'noumenal choice' coherent and its relation to time or timelessness, see Kant, *Religion within the Boundaries of Mere Reason*, pp. 55–56 (6.31–31; 6.43) and p. 72 (6.48).
22. Jordan Bell, 'Corruption and Autonomy: Is Heaven Our Kind of Place?' Sermon delivered to Sunday Evening Service, St Hugh's College Chapel, University of Oxford, 2000.
23. Kant, *Religion within the Boundaries of Mere Reason*, p. 68 (6.47); here in Part One of the *Religion* a gradual reform is also mentioned. But for an account of the nature of 'a gradual reform' in 'becoming a human being well-pleasing to God', see Part Three, p. 124 (6.117).
24. For Kant's reference to 'the change heart', which might be taken metaphorically, since no empirical heart exists; there is the question of how this heart could have a relation to time arises, see Kant, *Religion within the Boundaries of Mere Reason*, pp. 67 (6.47) and 92 (6.67).
25. Ibid., p. 72 (6.52). It is also interesting to note parallels between Kant's theory of '*homo Noumenon*, "whose change takes place in heaven"', in 'The End of All Things'(in *Religion within the Boundaries of Mere Reason and Other Writings*, pp. 200–201; 8.334–335) and C. S. Lewis' controversial theory of heaven as presented in *The Great Divorce* (London: Geoffrey Bles, 1946). For both Kant and Lewis,

human freedom which cannot be overridden by God is central.

26. Recall the passage quoted in Chapter 2 (endnote 20) here in *Kant and Theology* from Kant, *Critique of Pure Reason*, p. 475nᵃ (A552/B580).

27. Allen W. Wood, *Kant's Ethical Thought* (Cambridge: Cambridge University Press, 1999). This line of quotation inside of the quotation of Wood is from Kant, 'What does it mean to orient oneself in thinking?' in *Religion and Rational Theology*. Translated by Allen W. Wood (Cambridge: Cambridge University Press (8.144).

28. In this, Wood quotes from Kant, *Critique of Pure Reason*, A738/B766.

29. Henry E. Allison, 'Reflections on the Banality of (Radical) Evil: A Kantian Analysis', in Allison, *Idealism and Freedom: Essays on Kant's Theoretical and Practical Philosophy* (Cambridge: Cambridge University Press, 1996), pp. 177–181, reprinted in Maria Pia Lara, ed. *Rethinking Evil: Contemporary Perspectives* (Berkeley: University of California Press, 2001), pp. 94–99.

30. Allison, 'Reflections on the Banality of (Radical) Evil', in Maria Pia Lara, ed. *Rethinking Evil*, p. 95.

31. Daniel Whistler, 'Kant's *imitatio Christi*', *International Journal of Philosophy of Religion* 67:1 (2010), p. 31.

32. Kant, *Religion within the Boundaries of Mere Reason*, p. 84 (6:66).

33. Whistler, 'Kant's *imitatio Christi*', p. 31.

Conclusion

1. For a range of different criticisms of Kantian autonomy, see Onora O'Neill, *Bounds of Justice* (Cambridge: Cambridge University Press, 2000), pp. 29–49.

2. Seyla Benhabib, *Situating the Self: Gender, Community and Postmodernism in Contemporary Ethics* (London: Routledge, 1992), p. 163.

3. Feminists of various persuasions have treated Kant as an arch-enemy. He is feared and rejected by various feminist theorists because of his apparent view of women as passive by nature, as determined more by inclination than reason, and because of the consequent, Kantian view that women cannot be legitimate citizens, cannot be equal partners in marriage and cannot be capable of scholarship. Feminist critics in ethics question the very features of his moral religion which have been influential on those modern theorists who fear pervasive relativism and the unsettling movements in our post-modern age. That is, Kant establishes the authority of human reason alone, the importance of general rules for ethics and the universalizability principle for considering the morality of rational beings abstracted, supposedly, from any cultural or social context.

4. For some critical work on Kant in relation to the emotions and injustice (and gender), see Victor J. Seidler, Kant, *Respect and Injustice: The Limits of Liberal Moral Theory* (London: Routledge & Kegan Paul, 1986); and Victor J. Seidler, *Jewish Philosophy and Western Culture: A Modern Introduction* (London: I. B. Tauris & Co. Ltd., 2007).

5. Roughly, the analytic scrutinizes the role of truth in its principles (for example, of empirical causality) by unpacking or deducing the central concepts of pure practical reason; in contrast, the dialectic exposes the role of illusion by demonstrating how it is that human thinking continues to seek, while never being able to achieve, the totality of all conditions (that is the unconditioned). See Immanuel Kant, *Critique of Practical Reason*. Translated and edited by Mary Gregor, Introduction by Andrews Reath, *Cambridge Texts in the History of Philosophy* (Cambridge University Press, 1997).

6. Pamela Sue Anderson, 'On Loss of Confidence: Dissymmetry, Doubt, Deprivation in the Power to Act and (the Power) to Suffer', in Daniel Whistler, James Carter and Joseph Carlisle, eds. *Moral Powers, Fragile Beliefs: Essays in*

Moral and Religious Philosophy (London and New York: Continuum, 2010). Also, see Paul Ricoeur, *Freud and Philosophy*: An Essay on Interpretation. Translated by Denis Savage (New Haven, NJ and London: Yale University Press, 1970), pp. 45–46.

7. Pamela Sue Anderson, 'Canonicity and Critique: A Feminist Defence of a Post-Kantian Critique', *Literature and Theology: An International Journal of Religion, Theory and Culture*, vol. 13 (September 1999), 201–210; translated into Hungarian, '*Kanonisag es kritika: egy posztkantianus kritika feminista vedelme*', in *Korunk*, XI/5 (2000, Majus), 67–74. Note that Ricoeur is a good example of a continental philosopher who has given new value to Kant's account of autonomy. But rather than being bothered by the possible gendered nature of Kant's standards, he is concerned to reject – what is equally rejected by feminist critics – an overly formal or rigorous account of Kantian autonomy. See Paul Ricoeur, *Oneself as Another*. Translated by Kathleen Blamey (Chicago: University of Chicago Press, 1992), pp. 209–218.

8. Anderson, 'Canonicity and Critique', pp. 201–210.

9. For discussion of the ignorance of rational autonomy which has tended to arise for philosophers holding naïve empiricist theories of motivation and of rationality as exclusively instrumental, see Onora O'Neill, *Towards Justice and Virtue: A Constructive Account of Practical Reasoning* (Cambridge: Cambridge University Press, 1996), pp. 6 and 42–44.

10. For the significance for women philosophers and others in discovering what might seem peripheral in a philosophical text, see Michèle Le Doeuff, *The Philosophical Imaginary*. Translated by Colin Gordon (London: The Athlone Press, 1989).

11. An exception to both categories – of modern Kant scholarship and of feminist interpretations – is O'Neill, *Constructions of Reason: Explorations of Kant's Practical*

Philosophy (Cambridge: Cambridge University Press, 1989), pp. 105–106, 198, 213; also, see O'Neill, *Towards Justice and Virtue*, pp. 191–203. For a further reading of Kantian autonomy, see Ricoeur, *Oneself as Another*, pp. 273–283.

12. For an account of how Kant's thinking in the third *Critique* might be extended, see Marcia Moen, 'Feminist Themes in Unlikely Places: Re-reading Kant's *Critique of Judgment*', in Robin May Schott, ed. *Feminist Interpretations of Immanuel Kant* (University Park, PA: The Pennsylvania University Press, 1997), pp. 213–255.

13. Kant, *Religion within the Boundaries of Mere Reason*, p. 80 (6:61).

14. Kant, *Religion within the Boundaries of Mere Reason,* p. 81 (6:62).

15. Compare this to John Rawls, 'Themes in Kant's Moral Philosophy', in Samuel Freeman, ed. *John Rawls: Selected Papers* (Cambridge, MA: Harvard University Press, 1999), pp. 504–506.

16. Kant *Groundwork*, pp. 43–44 (4: 436).

17. O'Neill, *Constructions of Reasons*, pp. 148–162.

18. See Pamela Sue Anderson, 'Ricoeur's Reclamation of Autonomy: Unity, Plurality and Totality', in John Wall, William Schweiker and W. David Hall, eds. *Paul Ricoeur and Contemporary Moral Thought* (New York: Routledge, 2002), pp. 15–31.

19. Ricoeur, *Oneself as Another*, p. 276; cf. Anderson, 'Ricoeur's Reclamation of Autonomy'.

20. Thomas McCarthy, 'Enlightenment and the Idea of Public Reason', and Cooke, 'Questioning Autonomy', in Richard Kearney and Mark Dooley, eds. *Questioning Ethics: Contemporary Debates in Philosophy* (London: Routledge, 1999), respectively, pp. 164–180 and pp. 258–282.

21. Kant, *Critique of Pure Reason*. Translated and edited by Paul Guyer and Allen W. Wood (Cambridge: Cambridge University Press, 1997), p. 643 (A738 /B766); also see pp. 100–101 (Axi–xiii).

22. For a recent essay supporting this view, see McCarthy, 'Enlightenment and the Idea of Public Reason'.
23. David Jasper, *A Short Introduction to Hermeneutics* (Westminster John Knox Press, 2004).
24. Carol Gilligan, *In A Different Voice* (Cambridge, MA: Harvard University Press, 1982); cf. Ricoeur, *Oneself as Another*, p. 283n73.
25. Benhabib, 'The Generalized and the Concrete Other', in *Situating the Self*, pp. 148–177.
26. Young, 'Asymmetrical Reciprocity', pp. 38–59.
27. Ricoeur, *Oneself as Another*, pp. 219–221.
28. Benhabib, *Situating the Self;* and Maria Pia Lara, *Moral Textures: Feminist Narratives in the Public Sphere* (Cambridge: Polity Press, 1998), pp. 81, 84–87, 192, 193.
29. For another defense of Kant's kingdom of ends, see Christine Korsgaard, *Creating the Kingdom of Ends* (Cambridge: Cambridge University Press, 1995); and 'Introduction', in *Groundwork of the Metaphysics of Morals*, pp. xxix–xxx.
30. Immanuel Kant, *Critique of the Power of Judgment.* Translated by Paul Guyer and Eric Matthews (Cambridge: Cambridge University Press, 2000), p. 174 (5.294).
31. O'Neill, *Constructions of Reason*, pp. 25–26; cf. Kant, *Critique of Judgment*, pp. 151–152.
32. Kant, 'An Answer to the Question, What is Enlightenment?', p. 58.

Bibliography

Works by Immanuel Kant

The Standard German Edition

Kant, Immanuel, <u>Gesammelte Schriften</u>, Ausgabeder Königlich preussischen Akademie der Wissenschaften. Berlin: W. de Gruyter, 1900–.

Main Versions of Works by Kant

Critique of Pure Reason. Translated by Norman Kemp Smith. London: Macmillan, 1933 = the first Critique.

Critique of Practical Reason. Translated by Mary J. Gregor, in Immanuel Kant, Practical Philosophy. Translated and Edited by Mary J. Gregor. Cambridge: Cambridge University Press, 1996 = the second Critique.

Critique of the Power of Judgment. Translated by Paul Guyer and Eric Matthews and Edited by Paul Guyer. Cambridge: Cambridge University Press, 2000 = the third Critique.

Prolegomena to Any Future Metaphysics. Translated by Lewis White Beck. Indianapolis: The Bobbs-Merrill Co., 1950.

Opus Postumum. Translated by Eckart Förster and Michael Rosen and Edited by Eckart Förster. Cambridge: Cambridge University Press, 1993.

'An Answer to the Question: What Is Enlightenment?' in Immanuel Kant, Practical Philosophy. Translated and Edited by Mary J. Gregor. Cambridge: Cambridge University Press, 1996.

Groundwork of the Metaphysics of Morals, in Immanuel Kant, Practical Philosophy. Translated and Edited by Mary J. Gregor. Cambridge: Cambridge University Press, 1996.

The Metaphysics of Morals, in Immanuel Kant, *Practical Philosophy.* Translated and Edited by Mary J. Gregor. Cambridge: Cambridge University Press, 1996.

'On the Common Saying: That May Be Correct in Theory, But it is of No Use in Practice', in Immanuel Kant, *Practical Philosophy.* Translated and Edited by Mary J. Gregor. Cambridge: Cambridge University Press, 1996.

'Toward Perpetual Peace: A Philosophical Project', in Immanuel Kant, *Practical Philosophy.* Translated and Edited by Mary J. Gregor. Cambridge: Cambridge University Press, 1996.

Religion and Rational Theology. Translated and Edited by Allen W. Wood and George di Giovanni. Cambridge: Cambridge University Press, 1996.

'The Conflict of the Faculties'. Translated by Mary J. Gregor and Robert Anchor, in Immanuel Kant, *Religion and Rational Theology.* Cambridge: Cambridge University Press 1996, pp. 233–328.

'The End of All Things'. Translated by Allen W. Wood, in Immanuel Kant, *Religion and Rational Theology.* Cambridge: Cambridge University Press, 1996.

Lectures on Ethics. Translated by Louis Infield. New York: Harper Torchbooks, 1963.

Religion within the Boundaries of Mere Reason and Other Writings. Introduction by Robert Merrihew Adams. Translated and Edited by Allen Wood and George di Giovanni. Cambridge: Cambridge University Press, 1998, pp. 31–192.

Alternative Versions of Works by Kant

Critique of Pure Reason. Translated and Edited by Paul Guyer and Allen W. Wood. Cambridge: Cambridge University Press, 1998.

Critique of Practical Reason, trans. Lewis White Beck. Indianapolis: The Bobbs-Merrill Co., 1956.

Religion within the Limits of Reason Alone, trans. Theodore M. Greene and Hoyt H. Hudson. New York: Harper & Row, 1960.

Groundwork of the Metaphysic of Morals, trans. H. J. Paton. New York: Harper & Row, 1964; also, *The Moral Law: Kant's Groundwork of the Metaphysics of Morals*. Translated and Analysed by H. J. Paton. London: Hutchinson, 1951.

Lectures on Ethics. Translated by Peter Heath, Edited by Peter Heath and J. B. Schneewind. Cambridge: Cambridge University Press, 1997.

Works by Other Authors

Adams, Robert M., 'Involuntary Sins', *The Philosophical Review* 94 (1985): 3–31.

Adams, Robert M. and Adams, Marilyn M. (eds), *The Problem of Evil*. Oxford: Oxford University Press, 1990.

Allison, Henry E., *Kant's Transcendental Idealism: An Interpretation and Defense*. New Haven: Yale University Press, 1983.

Allison, Henry E., *Kant's Theory of Freedom*. Cambridge: Cambridge University Press, 1990.

Allison, Henry E., *Idealism and Freedom: Essays on Kant's Theoretical and Practical Philosophy*. Cambridge: Cambridge University Press, 1996.

Anderson, Pamela Sue, *Ricoeur and Kant: Philosophy of the Will*. Atlanta, GA: Scholars Press, 1993.

Anderson, Pamela Sue, 'Canonicity and Critique: A Feminist Defence of a Post-Kantian Critique', *Literature and Theology: An International Journal of Religion, Theory and Culture*, vol. 13 (September 1999): 201–210; translated into Hungarian, 'Kanonisag es kritika: egy posztkantianus kritika feminista vedelme', *Korunk*, XI/5 (2000, Majus): 67–74.

Anderson, Pamela Sue, 'Ricoeur's Reclamation of Autonomy: Unity, Plurality and Totality', in John Wall, William Schweiker and W. David Hall (eds), *Paul Ricoeur and Contemporary Moral Thought*. New York: Routledge, 2002, pp. 15–31.

Anderson, Pamela Sue, 'On Loss of Confidence: Dissymmetry, Doubt, Deprivation in the Power to Act and (the Power) to Suffer', in Joseph Carlisle, James Carter and Daniel Whistler (eds), *Moral Powers, Fragile Beliefs: Essays in Moral and Religious Philosophy*. London and New York: Continuum, 2010, chapter 4.

Arendt, Hannah, *Lectures on Kant's Political Philosophy*, Edited and with an Introduction by Ronald Beiner. Chicago: The University of Chicago Press, 1982.

Beck, Lewis White, *A Commentary on Kant's Critique of Practical Reason*. Chicago: The University of Chicago Press, 1960.

Bell, Jordan, 'Corruption and Autonomy: Is Heaven Our Kind of Place?' Sermon delivered at Sunday Evening Service, St Hugh's College Chapel, University of Oxford, Oxford, UK, October 2000.

Benhabib, Seyla, *Situating the Self: Gender, Community and Postmodernism in Contemporary Ethics*. London: Routledge, 1992.

Bennett, Jonathan, *Kant's Dialectic*. Cambridge: Cambridge University Press, 1974.

Broad, C. D., *Kant: An Introduction*. Cambridge: Cambridge University Press, 1978.

Byrne, Peter, *Kant on God*. Aldershot, Hants: Ashgate Publishing Ltd., 2007.

Carlisle, Joseph, Carter, James and Whistler, Daniel (eds), *Moral Power, Fragile Beliefs: Essays in Moral and Religious Philosophy*. New York and London: Continuum, 2010.

Carnois, Bernard, *The Coherence of Kant's Doctrine of Freedom*. Translated by David Booth. Chicago: The University of Chicago Press, 1987.

Carter, James, 'Moral Religion: Ethics, Hermeneutics and Life', D.Phil Thesis. University of Oxford, forthcoming.

Cooke, Maeve, 'Questioning Autonomy', in Richard Kearney and Mark Dooley (eds), *Questioning Ethics: Contemporary Debates in Philosophy*. London: Routledge, 1999, pp. 258–282.

Copleston, Frederick, *A History of Philosophy*, volume 6. *The Enlightenment: Voltaire to Kant*. London and New York: Continuum, 2003.

Cornell, Drucilla, *Moral Images of Freedom: A Future for Critical Theory*. Lanham, Maryland; and Plymouth, UK: Rowman & Littlefield Publishers, Inc., 2008.

Despland, Michel, *Kant on History and Religion*. Montreal: McGill-Queen's University Press, 1973.

Erb, Peter C. (ed.), *Pietists: Selected Writings*, with an Introduction by Peter C. Erb, and a Preface by F. Ernest Stoeffler. London: SPCK, 1983.

Firestone, Chris L. and Jacobs, Nathan, *In Defense of Kant's Religion*, Foreword by Nicholas Wolterstorff. Bloomington, IN: Indiana University Press, 2008.

Firestone, Chris L. and Palmquist, Stephen R. (eds), *Kant and the New Philosophy of Religion*. Bloomington, IN: Indiana University Press, 2006.

Gilligan, Carol, *In A Different Voice*. Cambridge, MA: Harvard University Press, 1982.

Greene, Theodore M., 'The Historical Context and Religious Significance of Kant's *Religion*', in Immanuel Kant, *Religion within the Limits of Reason Alone*. Translated by Theodore M. Greene and Hoyt H. Hudson. New York: Harper & Row, 1960, pp. ix–lxxviii.

Gregor, Mary, *Laws of Freedom: A Study of Kant's Method of Applying the Categorical Imperative in the Metaphysic der Sitten*. Oxford: Basil Blackwell, 1963.

Guyer, Paul, *Kant and the Experience of Freedom: Essays on Aesthetics and Morality*. Cambridge: Cambridge University Press, 1993.

Guyer, Paul, *Kant on Freedom, Law, and Happiness*. Cambridge: Cambridge University Press, 2000.

Guyer, Paul (ed.), *Kant's Groundwork of the Metaphysics of Morals: Critical Essays*. Lanham, NJ: Rowman & Littlefield, 1998.

Hampson, Daphne, 'Kant and the Present', in Pamela Sue Anderson (ed.), *New Topics in Feminist Philosophy of Religion: Contestations and Transcendence Incarnate*. Dordrecht; London; New York: Springer, 2010, pp. 147–162.

Hare, John, *The Moral Gap: Kantian Ethics, Human Limits and God's Assistance*. New York: Oxford University Press, 1996.

Haslanger, Sally, 'On Being Objective and Being Objectified', in Louise M. Antony and Charlotte Witt (eds), *A Mind of One's Own: Feminist Essays on Reason and Objectivity*. Oxford: Westview Press, 1993, pp. 85–126.

Herman, Barbara, *The Practice of Moral Judgment*. Cambridge, MA: Harvard University Press, 1993.

Herman, Barbara, 'Could It Be Worth Thinking About Kant on Sex and Marriage', in Louise M. Antony and Charlotte Witt (eds), *A Mind of One's Own: Feminist Essays on Reason and Objectivity*. Oxford: Westview Press, 1993, pp. 49–68.

Hill, Thomas E., Jr., *Dignity and Practical Reason in Kant's Moral Theory*. Ithaca, NY: Cornell University Press, 1992.

Hill, Thomas E., Jr., *Respect, Pluralism, and Justice: Kantian Perspectives*. Oxford: Oxford University Press, 2000.

Jasper, David, *A Short Introduction to Hermeneutics*. Louisville, KY: Westminster John Knox Press, 2004.

Kenyon, J. D., *Kant: The Limits of Experience*. Manuscript. University of Oxford, unpublished.

Kneller, Jane. *Kant and the Power of Imagination*. Cambridge: Cambridge University Press, 2007.

Korsgaard, Christine M., *Creating the Kingdom of Ends*. Cambridge: Cambridge University Press, 1996.

Korsgaard, Christine M., *The Sources of Normativity*. Cambridge: Cambridge University Press, 1996.

Kosch, Michelle, *Freedom and Reason in Kant, Schelling and Kierkegaard*. Oxford: Clarendon Press, 2006.

Kuehn, Manfred, *Kant: A Biography*. Cambridge: Cambridge University Press, 2001.

Langton, Rae, 'Feminism in Epistemology: Exclusion and Objectification', in Miranda Fricker and Jennifer Hornsby (eds), *The Cambridge Companion to Feminism in Philosophy*. Cambridge: Cambridge University Press, pp. 127–145.

Lara, Maria Pia, *Moral Textures: Feminist Narratives in the Public Sphere*. Cambridge: Polity Press, 1998.

Lara, Maria Pia (ed.), *Rethinking Evil: Contemporary Perspectives*. Berkeley and London: University of California Press, 2001.

Le Doeuff, Michèle, *The Philosophical Imaginary*. Translated by Colin Gordon. London: The Athlone Press, 1989; London: Continuum, 2002.

Le Doeuff, Michèle, 'Beauvoir the Mythoclast', and 'Panel Discussion with Michèle Le Doeuff', *Paragraph* 33:1 (2010): 90–104 and 105–124.

Lewis, C. S., *The Great Divorce*. London: Geoffrey Bles, 1946.

Lloyd, Genevieve, 'Feminism in the History of Philosophy: Appropriating the Past', in Miranda Fricker and Jennifer Hornsby (eds), *The Cambridge Companion to Feminism in Philosophy*. Cambridge: Cambridge University Press, 2000, pp. 245–263.

Matthews, H. E. [1969], 'Strawson on Transcendental Idealism', in Ralph C. S. Walker (eds), *Kant on Pure Reason*. Oxford Readings in Philosophy. Oxford: Oxford University Press, 1982, pp. 132–149.

McCarthy, Thomas, 'Enlightenment and the Idea of Public Reason', in Richard Kearney and Mark Dooley (eds), *Questioning Ethics: Contemporary Debates in Philosophy*. London: Routledge, 1999, pp. 164–180.

Mendus, Susan, 'The Practical and Pathological', in *Feminism and Emotion: Readings in Moral and Political Philosophy*. London: Macmillan Press, Ltd., 2000, pp. 43–54.

Michalson, Jr., Gordon E., *Fallen Freedom: Kant on Radical Evil and Moral Regeneration*. Cambridge: Cambridge University Press, 1990.

Michalson, Jr., Gordon E., *Kant and the Problem of God*. Oxford: Basil Blackwell, 1999.

Moen, Marcia, 'Feminist Themes in Unlikely Places: Re-reading Kant's *Critique of Judgment*', in Robin May Schott (ed.), *Feminist Interpretations of Immanuel Kant*. University Park, PA: The Pennsylvania University Press, 1997, pp. 213–255.

Moore, A. W., *Noble in Reason, Infinite in Faculty: Themes and Variations in Kant's Moral and Religious Philosophy.* London: Routledge, 2003.

Nussbaum, Martha C., 'Objectification', in *Sex and Social Justice.* Oxford: Oxford University Press, 1999, pp. 213–239.

O'Neill, Onora, *Constructions of Reason: Explorations of Kant's Practical Philosophy.* Cambridge: Cambridge University Press, 1989.

O'Neill, Onora, *Towards Justice and Virtue: A Constructive Account of Practical Reasoning.* Cambridge: Cambridge University Press, 1996.

O'Neill, Onora, 'Necessary Anthropomorphism and Contingent Speciesism' (Part II of 'Kant on Duties Regarding Non-rational Nature'), in *Proceedings of the Aristotelian Society* Supp. 72:1 (1998): 211–228.

O'Neill, Onora, *Bounds of Justice.* Cambridge: Cambridge University Press, 2000.

Rawls, John, 'Themes in Kant's Moral Philosophy', in Samuel Freeman (ed.), *John Rawls: Selected Papers.* Cambridge, MA: Harvard University Press, 1999, pp. 497–528.

Reardon, Bernard M. G., *Kant as Philosophical Theologian.* London: Macmillan, 1988.

Reath, Andrews, 'Kant's Theory of Moral Sensibility: Respect for the Moral Law and the Influence of Inclination', in *Kant-Studien* 80 (1989): 284–302.

Ricoeur, Paul, *Freedom and Nature: The Voluntary and the Involuntary.* Translated by Erazim Kohak. Evanston: Northwestern University Press, 1966.

Ricoeur, Paul, *Freud and Philosophy: An Essay on Interpretation.* Translated by Denis Savage. New Haven and London: Yale University Press, 1970.

Ricoeur, Paul, 'Freedom in the Light of Hope', trans. Robert Sweeney, in his *The Conflict of Interpretations: Essays in Hermeneutics.* Edited by Don Ihde. Evanston: Northwestern University Press, 1974.

Ricoeur, Paul, *Oneself as Another*. Translated by Kathleen Blamey. Chicago: The University of Chicago Press, 1992.

Rossi, Philip J. and Wreen, Michael (eds), *Kant's Philosophy of Religion Reconsidered*. Bloomington and Indianapolis: Indiana University Press, 1991.

Schneewind, J. B., 'Autonomy, Obligation, and Virtue: An Overview of Kant's Moral Philosophy', in Paul Guyer (ed.), *The Cambridge Companion to Kant*. Cambridge: Cambridge University Press, 1992, pp. 309–341.

Seidler, Victor J., *Kant, Respect and Injustice: The Limits of Liberal Moral Theory*. London: Routledge & Kegan Paul plc, 1986.

Seidler, Victor J., *Jewish Philosophy and Western Culture: A Modern Introduction*. London: I. B. Tauris & Co. Ltd., 2007.

Sherman, Nancy, *Making a Necessity of Virtue: Aristotle and Kant on Virtue*. Cambridge: Cambridge University Press, 1997.

Silber, John R., 'The Ethical Significance of Kant's *Religion*', in Immanuel Kant, *Religion within the Limits of Reason Alone*. Translated by Theodore M. Greene and Hoyt H. Hudson. New York: Harper & Row, 1960, pp. lxxix–cxxxiv.

Spener, Philip Jakob, *Pia desideria*. Translated, Edited and with an Introduction by Theodore G. Tappert. Philadelphia, PA: Fortress Press, 1964.

Strawson, P. F., *Bounds of Sense: An Essay on Kant's Critique of Pure Reason*. London: Methuen, 1966.

Uleman, Jennifer K., *An Introduction to Kant's Moral Philosophy*. Cambridge: Cambridge University Press, 2010.

Walker, Ralph C. S., *Kant*. London: Routledge & Kegan Paul, 1978.

Ward, Keith, *The Development of Kant's View of Ethics*. Oxford: Basil Blackwell, 1972.

Whistler, Daniel, 'Kant's *imitatio Christi*', *International Journal of Philosophy of Religion*, 67:1 (February 2010): 17–36.

Wilkerson, T. E., *Kant's Critique of Pure Reason*. Oxford: Clarendon Press, 1976.

Wolterstorff, Nicholas P., 'Conundrums in Kant's Rational Religion', in Philip J. Rossi and Michael Wreen (eds), *Kant's Philosophy of Religion Reconsidered*. Bloomington, IN: Indiana University Press, 1991, pp. 40–53.

Wolterstorff, Nicholas P., 'Is It Possible and Desirable for Theologians to Recover from Kant?' *Modern Theology*, 14, no. 1 (1998): 1–18.

Wood, Allen W., *Kant's Moral Religion*. Ithaca: Cornell University Press, 1970.

Wood, Allen W., *Kant's Rational Theology*. Ithaca: Cornell University Press, 1978.

Wood, Allen W., 'Kant's Compatibilism', in Allen W. Wood (ed.), *Self and Nature in Kant's Philosophy*. Ithaca: Cornell University Press, 1984, pp. 73–101.

Wood, Allen W., 'Kant's Deism', in Philip J. Rossi and Michael Wreen (eds), *Kant's Philosophy of Religion Reconsidered*. Bloomington, IN: Indiana University Press, 1991, pp. 1–21.

Wood, Allen W., 'Rational Theology, Moral Faith, and Religion', in Paul Guyer (ed.), *The Cambridge Companion to Kant*. Cambridge: Cambridge University Press, 1992.

Wood, Allen W., 'Kant on Duties Regarding Non-rational Nature', in *Proceedings of the Aristotelian Society* Supp. Vol. 72 (1998): 189–210.

Wood, Allen W., *Kant's Ethical Thought*. Cambridge: Cambridge University Press, 1999.

Wood, Allen W., *Kant*. Blackwell Great Minds series. Malden, MA and Oxford: Blackwell, 2005.

Young, Iris Marion, 'Asymmetrical Reciprocity: On Moral Respect, Wonder and Enlarged Thought', in *Intersecting Voices: Dilemmas of Gender, Political Philosophy and Policy*. Princeton, NY: Princeton University Press, 1997, pp. 38–59.

Index

Index

happiness v, 34, 56, 79
harness-maker 1, 3
heart 2, 101n. 24
heaven ix, 67–8, 70, 71,
    101n. 25
Herman, Barbara 97n. 34
hermeneutic 44–5, 46, 82–3,
    93n. 1
holy 27, 29, 36, 82
humanity 27, 29, 34, 57, 85
    human ix, 20, 34, 92n. 11
Hume, David 16

ideal 8, 30, 47–8, 61, 65, 81
    regulative 53, 65
idealism 11
    transcendental
        idealism 11–13, 17–28,
        31, 81, 91n. 5, 92n. 12
Immanuel 1
immortality 21, 58, 59, 61
imperative 27, 80–1
    categorical 27, 28, 32, 79,
        80, 86, 93n. 6
    formulations 79–80
inclination 28, 30–3, 35–7,
    40–3, 57, 67, 71,
    76–7, 103n. 3
individual 3, 15–16, 31, 47,
    71, 94n. 16
intelligible 30, 73
intuition 15, 56, 62, 64, 80
    forms of 15
island v, 20–1, 91–2n. 7

Jasper, David 44, 97n. 6

Kenyon, J. D. x
kingdom of ends 32, 34,
    80–1, 85–6, 106n. 29
knowledge v, 1–2, 12–14,
    36, 76, 89n. 2
    see also epistemology
    unknowable 92n. 11
Königsberg 1–7, 10
    Kaliningrad 10
Kuehn, Manfred 89n. 1

law 27, 31, 34, 37, 42, 80–1
    moral law 30, 36–7, 43,
    46, 56, 57, 61
Le Doeuff, Michèle 46,
    89n. 2
lie/lying 23, 41
limit 12, 20, 36, 46, 76–7, 80
Lloyd, Genevieve 45
Locke, John 13
lust 36–42, 46
Lutheran 2–3, 89n. 5

marriage 6, 46, 95n. 25,
    96n. 29, 103n. 3
mathematics 6, 11
maxim 7, 27, 39, 69–70,
    78–81, 83, 85
means 27–8, 32, 38
    'merely as a means' 27, 81
metaphor v, 6, 13
metaphysics ix, 6, 11, 13,
    16–17, 29, 44, 58
Michalson, Gordon E. 58,
    93n. 7, 99n. 21
Montefiore, Alan x

Index

understanding 15, 17, 21–2,
  24, 27, 30, 79, 85, 92n. 7
unity 79–80
universal(ity) 15, 27, 31, 34,
  42, 80–1

virtue 34, 56

Wesley, John 3, 90n. 6
Whistler, Daniel 72–3,
  102n. 31
will 13, 23, 27, 31, 43, 68, 70
  free will *see* freedom
  good will *see* good

Wolff, Christian 5
Wöllner, Johann
  Christoph 8–9
Wood, Allen W. 34, 71,
  89n. 5, 90n. 9, 93n. 7,
  97n. 3
world 13–15, 17, 20,
  23, 27, 30, 32, 37,
  44, 52–3, 55–7, 67,
  73, 78
  possible worlds 51
  of sense 27, 30, 78
  of understanding 27, 30
  see also two-world